Gold Fish
and
Silver Kisses

Gold Fish and Silver Kisses

how to talk to children about God

Linda Carol Masters

Sawdust Publishing

Copyright © 2001 Linda Carol Masters
2nd edition © 2006

All rights reserved. No part of this book may be reproduced or transmitted in any form or by any means, electronic or mechanical, including photocopying, recording or by any information storage and retrieval system, without permission in writing from:

Sawdust Publishing
P.O. Box 8328
Huntsville, TX 77340

This book was printed in the U.S.A.

Library of Congress Number:
    2001096600

ISBN: Paperback
    0-9768329-1-7

Biblical selections from the *Life Application Study Bible* Wheaton, Ill.: Tyndale House, 1996.

Table of Contents

Acknowledgments xvi
Dedication xvii
Introduction xvii

For Any Time

1. **It's Contagious!** (Acts 2:46-47) 1
   Theme: Let others catch Jesus from you.
2. **Reflections Of God's Glory** (Genesis 1:26-27) 4
   Theme: Everything comes from God.
3. **God Can Mend A Broken Heart** (Jeremiah 20:7-12) 7
   Theme: During our times of sadness, we learn to trust God.
4. **It's Easy To Burst A Bubble** (Proverbs 11:9) 9
   Theme: Words are one of the most powerful forces in the world.
5. **The Key To Death And Life** (II Corinthians 4:16-18,
      Proverbs 12:28) 11
   Theme: Jesus is the key to life, the key to death,
   and the key to heaven.
6. **Which Way?** (Psalms 25:8-10) 13
   Theme: Let God be your compass.
7. **The Gift Of Grace** (Ephesians 1:7-8) 16
   Theme: God gives you the gift of forgiveness — grace.
8. **Things Change** (Psalms 59:10) 19
   Theme: In an ever-changing world, God is a constant.
9. **The Rainbow — The Promise** (Genesis 6:14, 9:8-17) 21
   Theme: Be a pleasure to God.
10. **Is Your Conscience Clear?** (Luke 16:13) 24
    Theme: Make God the master of your conscience.
11. **Feed My Sheep, Little Lambs** (John 21:15-17) 27
    Theme: A little kindness goes a long way.
12. **Handy Hands** — a good Samaritan story —
    (Luke 10:25-37) 30
    Theme: Use your hands wisely; use them to please God

13. **Spread A Little Sunshine** (Matthew 5:38-48) 33
    Theme: Share your Christian joy with your friends and your enemies.
14. **Lost And Found** — a prodigal son story —
    (Luke 15:11-24,32) 36
    Theme: The difference between bitterness and joy is
      our being able to forgive.
15. **God's Greatest Magic** (Mark 12:30-31) 39
    Theme: What you do with love will determine the course of
      your life.
16. **God's Rules — God's Rock** (Matthew 7:24-27) 41
    Theme: Rules are for our own good.
17. **Don't Blame The Shepherd** (Psalm 23) 44
    Theme: If you walk with God, he will guide you all the
      way to heaven.
18. **Figs, In-Deed!** (Luke 13:1-9) 47
    Theme: God wants us to be useful and to serve a purpose.
19. **De-Bark** — the Zacchaeus story — (Luke 19:1-10) 50
    Theme: Jesus can peel off ugly behavior.
20. **Armed With God's Trumpet** (Judges 6:1-7:25) 53
    Theme: Don't be surprised when God wants to use you.
21. **Daniel And Some Hungry Lions** — from the lions' point
    of view — (Daniel 6:1-7:4) 56
    Theme: Talk to God everyday.
22. **Wrong Is Never Right** (Psalms 51:10) 59
    Theme: There is never a right way to do the wrong thing.
23. **Give What You Are** (Matthew 19:16-22, I Timothy 6:18) . . .62
    Theme: Hold on to innocence, faith, and love, but give
      what you are.
24. **Jesus, Be My Umbrella** (Matthew 4:1-10) 65
    Theme: Jesus can protect you from temptation.
25. **We Come In Different Flavors** (John 13:34) 68
    Theme: No matter our color on the outside,
      we're all the same color on the inside.
26. **Nothing About Mad Feels Good** (Psalms 37:8-9) 70
    Theme: Ask God to replace your anger with peace.

27. **God's Traffic Rules — The Big Ten** (Exodus 20) 73
    Theme: God expects us to try our best.
28. **Life Has Its Ups And Downs** (James 1:2-3) 76
    Theme: Sometimes bad things turn out to be good things.
29. **Bless Others With A Smile** (Matthew 5:7) 79
    Theme: God wants us to bring joy to others.
30. **Holy Ghost!** (Acts 2:1-13, Matthew 28:20) 81
    Theme: The Holy Ghost is the Spirit of God.
31. **Does God Really Talk?** (Isaiah 58:9) 84
    Theme: God really does talk.
32. **Answers On Board** (Luke 18:1-8, Colossians 4:2) 87
    Theme: Learn to listen and watch for God's answers.
33. **A Dirty Story** — parable of the four soils —
    (Matthew 13:1-23) 90
    Theme: Plant yourself in God's love and care,
        and you will grow into a strong, productive Christian.
34. **The Doer And The Talker** — parable of the two sons —
    (Matthew 21:28-32, Luke 3:8) 93
    Theme: Repentance has two sides to it.
35. **Be Prepared** — parable of the ten virgins —
    (Matthew 25:1-13) 96
    Theme: We don't know what is in our future;
        be prepared with Jesus.
36. **A Talent Of Talent** — parable of the loaned money —
    (Matthew 25: 14-30) 99
    Theme: Be the best YOU that you can be.
37. **The Crown Of Life** (Mark 10:32-34) 102
    Theme: Your future is the crown of life if you trust
        and believe in Jesus.
38. **God's Amazing Guidance** (Psalms 35:4) 105
    Theme: In life there will be obstacles.
39. **Of Faith And Frogs** (Exodus 7-11, Psalms 11:4) 107
    Theme: Don't be stubborn when it comes to God.
40. **Storing Memories** (Deuteronomy 6:5, Matthew 22:37,
    Mark 12:30, Luke 10:27) 110
    Theme: Fill your memory store with Godly things.

41. **Heart Of Gold** (Isaiah 1:1-20, Matthew 15:8-9) 112
    Theme: God doesn't like fakes.
42. **Wisdom And Common Sense** (Proverbs 4:7) 115
    Theme: Wisdom and common sense will keep you
        on the right path.
43. **Giving God** (Acts 4:31-35) 117
    Theme: Sharing feels good.
44. **Making Memories With God** (Joshua 4) 119
    Theme: Who is Lord of your life?
45. **Oh, My God** (Matthew 11:25-28,Psalms 46:10). 122
    Theme: Belief in God must be more than an idea
46. **Oh, My Goodness** (Titus 1:15, Psalms 119:9) 125
    Theme: Look for the good in others instead of the bad.
47. **For Big Mistakes** (Luke 6:37) 127
    Theme: God allows us to make mistakes so we can
        see our blessings.
48. **Strength Of Fortune** (Nehemiah 8: 10) 130
    Theme: God's word and God's joy can be your strength.
49. **The Right Kind** (Matthew 5-9) 132
    Theme: Sometimes it is better to be kind than right.
50. **Fall For Goodness' Sake** (I Peter 3:16) 134
    Theme: Your reputation isn't so much what you
        stand for — it's what you fall for.
51. **A Patient Of Patience** (Psalms 46:10) 137
    Theme: Learn to be patient. God is in control.
52. **A New Pair Of Eyes** (Acts 9:1-18) 140
    Theme: Look at the world through the eyes of love.
53. **The Problems Of Roads** (John 16:29-33) 143
    Theme: Put Jesus in your driver's seat.
54. **Honorably Humble** (Luke 14:7-11) 145
    Theme: God will honor you for loving and helping others.
55. **One Kangaroo** (Genesis 3:9) 147
    Theme: You can't hide from God.
56. **The Color Of Truth** (Mark 7:1 -8, 14-15, 21-23) 150
    Theme: God looks for goodness, not just good works.
57. **Store My Treasures In Heaven** (Matthew 6:19-24) 152

Theme: Store God's word in your heart, and
you'll be storing treasures in heaven.
58. **Rocks And Cornerstones** (Matthew 2:33-43, Isaiah 28:6) ..155
Theme: Build your life on the foundation of Jesus
through prayer and commitment.
59. **Simply Believe** (Matthew 18:1-6, Mark 10:13-16) 158
Theme: Always keep your childlike faith in God.
60. **I'm In A Fix** (Philippians 4:6) 160
Theme: Look at your own faults before you look for
faults in others.
61. **Spouse Alert** (Psalms 32:8) 162
Theme: Ask God to put the right people in your life.
62. **Human Nature** (Romans 4:23-5:11) 164
Theme: Jesus gave you the honor of becoming God's child.
63. **I'm Sure!** (Hebrews 11:1) 167
Theme: Faith in God shouldn't change with the situation.
64. **Clothed** (Colossians 3:12) 169
Theme: Clothe yourself in the goodness of Jesus.
65. **Look Through The Eyes Of Faith** (Matthew 18:10-11) 171
Theme: God has blessed you with your own angel.
66. **Spend Promises Wisely** (Genesis 9:8-17) 174
Theme: Take promises seriously; make promises seriously.
67. **Sadness Or Gladness** (Psalms 118:24) 177
Theme: Be glad for what you have.
68. **Standing On Standard** (I Samuel 16:17) 180
Theme: Measure your standards by God's, not man's.
69. **God In Front — Jesus Inside** (Proverbs 3:6) 183
Theme: Put God first in everything you do.
70. **Looking For Joy** (Nehemiah 8:10) 185
Theme: You will be as happy or sad as you choose to be.
71. **Love Your Neighbor** (Luke 10:25-37) 187
Theme: Be kind to all your neighbors, even the
ones you don't like.

For Special Services

72. **Holy Communion** (Matthew 26:26-29) 190
    Theme: Taking communion is one of the most
          special things we get to do as Christians.
73. **The Lifetime Bath** — baptism — (Luke 3:7-22) 193
    Theme: Don't take the love of God for granted.
74. **A Little Fish And A Little Faith** (John 6:1-11) 196
    Theme: Give what you can, and let Jesus figure
          out what to do with it.

For Special Occasions

75. **Let's Talk About The Bible** — could be used the Sunday
    before Vacation Bible School or anytime —
    (Psalms 119:105) 199
    Theme: The Bible is about God's promises that have come
          to pass and those we can still look forward to.
76. **The Wind And The Spirit** — could be used on a holiday
    where the flag is celebrated — (John 20:29) 202
    Theme: Things unseen can be very powerful — like the wind
          and the Holy Spirit.
77. **Heart Full Of Love** — Valentine's Day — (Luke 6:45) 205
    Theme: Let God determine your destiny.
78. **Lend A Helping Hand** — Halloween — (I Timothy 5:4) ...207
    Theme: Lend a helping hand, and you will receive the blessing.
79. **The Greatest Gift Of All** — Mother's Day —
    (I Corinthians 13:8) 209
    Theme: Give your mother your love. It's the greatest gift of all.
80. **Operating Instructions** — Mother's Day — (Exodus 20:12) 211
    Theme: Honor your mother.
81. **Taping What Is Torn** — Father's Day or anytime —
    (Luke 15) 214
    Theme: God can tape your life back together when
          it has been torn all apart.

For Advent, Christmas, And Epiphany — The Christmas Season

82. **Make A Joyful Noise** — for the Sunday the choir sings special Christmas music — (Psalms 100:1-2) 217
    Theme: Music can polish your soul.
83. **Rejoice, Rejoice** — for the third Sunday of Advent or anytime during the Christmas Season — (Matthew 1:21) 220
    Theme: Lead a life that lends beauty and grace to Jesus.
84. **Legend Of The Poinsettia** (Song of Solomon 8:7) 223
    Theme: God can turn your love into something beautiful.
85: **Legend Of The Candy Cane** (Luke 2:1-11) 226
    Theme: Keep "Christ" in Christmas.
86. **The Light Of The World** — could be used for Christmas Eve (Luke 2:1-20, John 12:46) 229
    Theme: Jesus came to this world to be our light in the darkness.
87. **An Eye On God,** for the Sunday before New Year's Day (Psalms 57:7-11) 232
    Theme: Keep an eye on God, and he will keep an eye on you.
88. **Gold, Frankincense, And Myrrh** — Epiphany or Christmas time (Matthew 2:1 1) 235
    Theme: Find ways to honor Jesus.
89. **Who Were Those Guys?** — Epiphany or Christmas time (Matthew 2:1-12) 238
    Theme: The Three Kings were wise; they came to worship Jesus.

For Palm Sunday, Easter, And Pentecost

90. **Make It A Holy Week** — Palm Sunday — (I Peter 1:15) ...241
    Theme: Christians need to be mindful of the events that led to the cross.
91. **It's All In God's Hands** — Palm Sunday — (Mark 11:1-11) 244
    Theme: Sometimes our greatest gifts from God are when he says no.

92. **A Kiss For Silver** — Easter Sunday — (Luke 22) 247
    Theme: No amount of money is worth more than love.
93. **The Lamb Of God** — Easter Sunday — (I Peter 1:13) 250
    Theme: Easter is about new life from death.
94. **Pentecost** — Pentecost Sunday — (Acts 2: 1-6, 25) 253
    Theme: Allow the Holy Spirit to keep you fired up in faith.

For Trinity Sunday, Thanksgiving And Christ The King Sunday

95. **Soul Custody** — on the meaning of baptism and
    The Trinity (Matthew 3:13-17) 256
    Theme: The Trinity is the team that adopts your soul.
96. **Thanksgiving, What's That About?** (I Chronicles 16:8) 259
    Theme: Be aware of your blessings, and then be thankful.
97. **Giving God Some Thanks** (Luke 17:11-19, Psalms 92:1) ...262
    Theme: Do you remember to say, "Thank you, God?"
98. **In The Names Of Jesus** — Christ the King Sunday
    (John 18:33-37, Daniel 7:14) 265
    Theme: Let Jesus be your life-saver.

For Out Of The Ordinary

99. **Bittersweet** — for when a pastor is leaving or retiring —
    (Hebrews 5:4) 268
    Theme: Saying good-by.
100. **Gone Fishing** — for a pastor's first Sunday in your
    church (Matthew 4:18-22) 271
    Theme: Jesus has a fishing job for you.
101. **9 - 1 - 1** — terrorist attack on America —
    (Romans 5:1-11) 274
    Theme: God's power is behind America because his
    son lives in the hearts of America.

About the Author 277

Acknowledgments

To the precious children of the First United Methodist Church in Huntsville, Texas, I owe my gratitude. Because of you I have seen and felt God in a whole new way. The blessing I receive when I see you scurrying down the aisle to hear about God, is more than I could ever give back. My love goes out to each of you.

Terry Murray, Lottie Harrison, and Missy Certa, thank you for your encouragement, your inspiration, your friendship and love, and for all the times you listened. Kathleen Chance, MY librarian, thank you for knowing where to find EVERYTHING and then helping me look. Sylvia Bell, thank you for tokens I have used for the children, and Betty Bruce, for the books.

Ethel Hollowman, thank you for finding the perfect scripture verses for me when I couldn't, and Scottie Roberts, thank you for sending me a sermon idea just when I needed one. Oh, for the kindness of strangers!

To my parents, Mary Maude and Bill Bolton, thank you for instilling in me the confidence to try though I might fail, stand though I might fall, and pursue my dreams though I might never see them come true. For I have found that it is in the trying and the standing and the dreaming that life's most valuable lessons take hold. Thank you for giving God to me.

Luke Masters, my son, thank you for allowing me to use stories about you in this book and for reaching the place in my heart where unconditional love abides.

Doug Masters, husband and soul-mate, you are the reason I could do any of this. You are my hero and my special gift from God that I cherish with all that is in me. I love you.

Dedication

*For **GOD**
and
Jim Dwigans*

Introduction

When I began doing children's sermons, my biggest concern, other than nerves, was trying to put God to the children in a way they could understand. However, I learned quickly that children understand God better than anyone because they put no limits on him. They simply believe. I came to realize that it was not my job to persuade them to have faith. It was my job to open up the possibilities of their faith and to expand their knowledge of God's gifts, promises, and words, to help them store scriptures in their memory banks, and to incorporate God's word in their lives.

The lessons are not in any particular order, so I have listed a theme under each title, with the scriptures it was based on, in the Table of Contents as well as in each lesson. The holiday and special occasion lessons are grouped together, but you will see that even those can be used as generic lessons with the omission of a sentence or two. I have written the lessons in this book the way I presented them to my church children with one exception. I presented each lesson using the **"sermon ending"** where I gave each child and the pastor a token or treat to help them remember its main idea. For this book I added a **"devotional ending"** as an option so that the same message and theme of the lesson could be given without a token or treat. I realized that by doing that, the lessons could be used as devotionals for Christian academies and schools, Vacation Bible School, Sunday School, chapel services, or as family or individual devotionals that children as well as adults could use.

As for the tokens and treats, I have made them, bought them, and have had some given to me. An example of a token I've given was for the lesson, "Life has its Ups and Downs." I gave each child a yo-yo. I found them at Dollar Tree, four to a package, for a dollar. They weren't yo-yos that would help them win a yo-yo contest, but that wasn't the idea. The idea was to give them something to help them remember that particular lesson. It worked because a year after I gave the yo-yos, a little boy told me he still had his and what it served to remind him of.

Most of the tokens I bought can be purchased from the **Oriental Trading Company Catalog** which can be ordered by calling **1-800-228-2269**, or you can shop online at www.oriental.com. I found many of the items at a dollar store named **Dollar Tree**. Card and party stores where party favors can be found, Walmart, or other discount stores are also wonderful places to shop for the types of items I give the children. Some of the items I have given my church children were things I made like cookies, book marks, or rainbows made out of the rim of a paper plate. I've even pulled sycamore leaves from my tree and picked up sycamore bark from the ground for a lesson about Zacchaeus. Craft books are wonderful places to get ideas for tokens to make for the children. A book I have used a lot and have mentioned under those sermons is **"Bible Fun For Everyone" ISBN 1-56231-344-4, phone (503) 266-9102, fax (503) 266-8749, e-mail www.hotp.com.** I have solicited help from people when the project required more time than my busy schedule allowed for me to do it alone. Places to look for help are nursing homes, senior centers, Sunday school departments, co-workers, friends, students (if you are a teacher), and family. Most people just don't mind helping someone make a little project for a child. If you decide to give tokens or treats, you may just want to do it once a month instead of every week, and use the devotional endings the rest of the time, or whatever works for you.

One point I want to strongly encourage is presentation. If you choose to give tokens, try to use interesting boxes, bags, cartons, pouches, etc., to carry them in. It delights the children and piques the curiosity of everyone, even the adults. Also, I'd like to mention delivery. It is important to practice your delivery of the lesson out loud. Present it to the children — not the congregation. The children need to be your focus and your intent. The congregation will understand and even be supportive of that. They take pleasure in watching the children become absorbed in the Spirit of God. I try to memorize the lesson for each week, but in case I get sidetracked, I do carry the lesson up with me to refer to.

Don't be surprised at how God will help you with your endeavor to minister to children. His help is amazing! It comes through family, friends, and strangers. It comes through ideas and unexpected discoveries. It comes in blessings.

Keep in mind that you are sharing God with children, so try your best. When you give God your best effort and seal it with your best intentions, he will confirm his approval with guidance and blessings. He will convict your heart with a passion that screams, **"I can do this!"** and you will learn, as I have learned, you simply can't out-give God.

#1
It's Contagious!
Based on Acts 2:25, 46-47
(the Holy Spirit)

THEME: Let others catch Jesus from you.

Have you ever been sick? I have too. Sometimes when you get sick, it's because someone you have been around was sick, and you catch the sickness from them. That happens when the sickness is contagious. CONTAGIOUS. Say that word for me — CONTAGIOUS. That can be a spooky word if you are talking about the flu or the measles or the chicken pox.

There was a second grade school teacher with a child in her class who got the chicken pox. That's a sickness where you have fever, and blisters pop out all over your body. It makes you feel bad, and it is contagious. Before long, a couple of other children in the class got the chicken pox, and then some other children did. A little boy named Michael went up to the teacher and said, "You know, there's so many kids absent, I think we ought to just call school off for a while and stay home." The teacher said, "That wouldn't be a bad idea. I'm sure glad you haven't gotten the chicken pox." Michael replied, "Oh, I won't be getting them. We get our chickens at Safeway." (Safeway is a grocery store.)

Yes, a sickness that is contagious is a bad thing, but other things can be contagious that are good things — like the Holy Spirit for example. In the book of Acts from the Bible, it tells us that the apostles, the first followers of Jesus, ate together, prayed together, and worshiped together, and the Holy Spirit came over them. Soon other people caught the Holy Spirit from them, and then others caught it from them, and it wasn't long before thousands of people had it!

The Holy Spirit — that is not a sickness — that is the power of Jesus filling up your life. And when the Holy Spirit fills you up, you become contagious with it. Then the people around you can catch it, especially if you tell them about it. Sharing Jesus with others — that's something to spread around no matter where you get your chicken.

Bible Verse:

The Bible verse today comes from **Acts 2:25**. You say after me: **"I know the Lord is always with me. He is helping me. God's mighty power supports me."**

Spread that around. Let others know that you love Jesus, and he loves you. Then you will be contagious in a good way. Let someone catch Jesus from you.

Sermon Ending:

I have a necklace for each of you today with a Christian symbol on it. Perhaps when you wear it, someone will ask you about it, and you can tell them that you are contagious with the Holy Spirit.

Devotional Ending:

CONTAGIOUS — that's not such a spooky word after all.

Prayer:

Now, bow your head, close your eyes, and let's talk to God. You say after me: **"Dear God, Make me contagious with the**

Holy Spirit. Let others catch Jesus from me. Amen."

(I found the Christian symbols in a package at Hobby Lobby — a chain of stores — and strung each on a colorful satin cord. However, there are some cross necklaces in the Oriental Trading Catalog *that have "Jesus Loves Me" written on them that would also be great.)*

#2
Reflections Of God's Glory
Based on Genesis 1:26-27
(the creation)

THEME: Everything comes from God.

Have you ever thought about what a fantastic imagination God has? Well, let's think about it for a moment. God thought up everything in the world and around the world. He even thought up the world! He thought up day and night. He thought up the oceans and all that is in them. He thought up dry land and everything that is on the land. He thought up you.

Some people question all that. For example, there was a team of scientists who decided they could and should create a human being, a person, without God's help. One day, one of those scientists walked outside the science laboratory where he worked and stood in the middle of the flower garden in front of the building. He looked up to the heavens and very proudly he shouted, "Where are you, God? Can you hear me? My name is Dr. Franklin Edison, and I just wanted you to know that we don't need you down here anymore. We have discovered a way to create human beings with no help from you and no help from nature. You are outdated, God. You are obsolete."

To Dr. Franklin Edison's surprise, God spoke back. He said to the scientist, **"Can you take some dirt and create a man as I did?"**

The scientist thought for a minute and said, "From dirt?" He bent over and scooped up a handful of dirt from the ground. Then very smugly he replied, "Yes, in time I can take dirt and create a man."

God took a deep breath and blew the dirt from Dr. Franklin Edison's hand and said, **"Get your own dirt."** *(Presenter should pretend to scoop up dirt when the scientist did, then blow the dirt away when God did in the story. The microphone makes it sound more "Godly.")*

You see, everything we have to use on this earth was put here by God, so whatever we make or create and no matter how smart we think we have become, we must remember that it all comes from God.

The Bible tells us that God created man and woman in his own image. That means each of you are a reflection of God's glory — each full of promise. On the day you were born, God planted inside you an imagination. Your best hope is to use your imagination to reflect God's character through love, patience, forgiveness, kindness, and faithfulness.

Bible Verse:

The Bible verse today comes from **Genesis 1:27**. You say after me: **"God created man in his own image."**

Dr. Franklin Edison wanted to be like God in a sense. He wanted to create and be smart and all-knowing, and there is nothing wrong with that. But he lost sight of one very important thing: anything he could ever imagine or make or create is *because of God.* So, as you live your life, let your imagination run wild: invent, create, make new and wonderful things. But always remember this: *everything comes from God.*

Sermon Ending:

I brought each of you some of God's dirt today that has been mixed with a little of God's magic. Put it somewhere so that you will see it everyday. Hopefully it will inspire you to take the things of this earth and with the magic and imagination God has planted inside you, strive to be the best reflection of God's glory that you can be.

Devotional Ending:

The next time you go outside to play, scoop up some of God's dirt in your hand. Put it in a container, and keep it where you will see it everyday. Hopefully it will inspire you to take the things of this earth and with the magic and imagination God has planted inside you, strive to be the best reflection of God's glory that you can be.

Prayer:

Now, bow your head, close your eyes, and let's talk to God. You say after me: **"Dear God, Thank you for everything! Amen."**

(I bought some plastic spice/desk-supplies type jars that came four to a pack for one dollar at Dollar Tree. They had colorful plastic push lids. I went down to a creek that runs through our property and dug up some sand. I then mixed the sand with some glitter and filled the jars.)

#3

God Can Mend A Broken Heart
Based on Jeremiah 17:7, 20:7-12

THEME: During our times of sadness, we learn to trust God.

As you go through life, you will experience all kinds of feelings and emotions. The feeling I want to talk to you about today is sadness. Have any of you ever been sad? Sure you have. It is a common human emotion that everyone feels at one time or another. Sometimes we are so sad that we cry. Being able to cry is really a wonderful thing. It is God's way of letting our sadness drain out of us. Sometimes we cry until we are empty of the sadness, and sometimes it's just enough so that we can deal with it better.

It helps if we talk about our sadness to someone, but do you know what helps get rid of our sadness better than anything? God. God can take a person's sadness and do the most wonderful things with it. God can turn sadness into a lesson about how to live and behave better. God can take our sadness and teach us to be more careful in our choices. God can turn sadness into a blessing by teaching us understanding and patience and how to be brave. Through our times of sadness, we learn to depend on God and trust him. Depending on and trusting in God is what

makes good and strong Christians.
Bible Verse:

The Bible verse today comes from **Jeremiah 17:7**. You say after me: **"Blessed is the man who trusts in the Lord and has made the Lord his hope and confidence."**

It's normal to feel sad sometimes. Things will happen in your life that will break your heart. But remember this: God made your heart and he can fix it when it is sad or even broken by hurt feelings. For that to happen, all you have to do is ask for God's help. It may take a minute or a long, long time, but God has his reasons for everything, and that is where trust comes in.

Sermon Ending:

I brought each of you a Band-Aid today. It's not your usual kind of Band-Aid like you would put on a cut or a wounded knee. It's a chocolate Band-Aid that can go inside your body where sadness can be. When you eat your Band-Aid, remember that God can go down inside you and heal your sadness. He can mend your broken heart.

Optional Sermon Ending:

I brought each of you a Band-Aid today. Let it remind you that God can protect you while you are healing from sadness. God can mend your broken heart.

Devotional Ending:

Think of a time when someone put a Band-Aid on you for a cut or a skinned knee. It protected your hurt place while it was healing. God can protect your heart like that until it has healed from sad or hurt feelings.

Prayer:

Now, bow your head, close your eyes, and let's talk to God. You say after me: **"Dear God, Whenever I am sad, heal me with your divine power. Amen."**

(I found chocolate Band-Aids at World Market. If you use regular Band-Aids, I suggest at least a 1" size.)

#4

It's Easy To Burst A Bubble
Based on Proverbs 11:9

THEME: Words are one of the most powerful forces in the world.

Have you ever heard the expression, *"He burst my bubble?"* It means that someone hurt your feelings, or that someone caused you to be disappointed.

One way to burst someone's bubble is with words. There's another expression you may have heard, and it goes *"Sticks and stones may break my bones, but words will never hurt me."* The truth is, words can hurt people terribly. They may not break bones, but words can break hearts.

Words are one of the most powerful forces in the world. They can bring about love, or they can cause hatred. Words can offer kindness, or they can hand out meanness. Words can bring about peace; words can cause nations to go to war. Words can foster happy feelings, and words can burst somebody's bubble.

Bursting a bubble is not a difficult thing to do. In fact, I brought some bubbles with me to show you just how delicate and fragile bubbles are. *(Presenter will blow bubbles from a bottle of "Bubble-Stuff" or a similar type product. Ask children to pop them.)* It's not that hard to burst a bubble, is it?

Bible Verse:

The Bible verse today comes from **Proverbs 11:9.** You say after me: **"Evil words destroy. Godly skills rebuilds."**

Sermon Ending:

The Bible also tells us in Proverbs, "A good man thinks before he speaks; the evil man pours out evil words without a thought." I brought each of you a bottle of bubbles to take with you. When you blow these bubbles, remember that they are fragile and easy to burst just like feelings.

Devotional Ending:

The Bible also tells us in Proverbs, "A good man thinks before he speaks; the evil man pours out evil words without a thought." Remember that feelings are as fragile and easy to burst as feelings. Be careful and mindful of what you say.

Prayer:

Now, bow your head, close your eyes, and let's talk to God. You say after me: **"Dear God, Help me to not hurt people with my words. Help me to show kindness toward others when I speak. Amen."**

(Don't fudge. Get the regular sized bottles of bubbles and not the little kind now used for weddings. The Sunday I did this lesson, there were bubbles floating all around the outside of the church after the service. The children loved them, and the adults got a treat just seeing all those beautiful bubbles floating in the air. You can buy bottles of bubbles in packets at dollar stores or through the Oriental Trading Catalog. *It was a magical few moments for everyone.)*

#5
The Key To Death And Life
Based on 2 Corinthians 4:16-18 and Proverbs 12:28
(about death)

THEME: Jesus is the key to life, the key to death, and the key to heaven.

I love life! Don't you? Think about it. You get a brand new day to experience every time you get out of bed in the mornings, and there are so many things we can do with it. We can learn, we can interact with other people, we can work and play, laugh and cry, eat and rest, love and hate, have good times and bad times, win and lose, feel brave and feel scared.

Life — I love it! I love being on this earth and waking up to fresh new days and brand new beginnings, but my life won't go on forever. Just like everyone else, I will die someday. Death is not something we like to think about even though it is a fact of life. Death is THE END — final — over — done with — unless you are a Christian. If you are a Christian, death is a brand new beginning.

Death is when God takes your soul, your feelings, your love, your thoughts, your spirit and moves them out of your body and into a brand new and perfect one. You get to move into heaven where there is no losing or tears or hate or anger or fear. There is only peace, love, and joy.

Death is the doorway between earth and heaven. It is all part of God's plan. Life on earth — then life in heaven. The key to that door is held by Jesus. He has the key that unlocks our doorway into heaven.

Love life! Enjoy it! Make the best of it, but for heaven's sake, don't leave out Jesus. He is the one you want to see when death calls on you.

Bible Verse:

The Bible verse today comes from **Proverbs 12:28**. You say after me: **The path of the Godly leads to life. So why fear death?**

The Bible tells us in 2nd Corinthians that we can look forward to our heavenly bodies and our home in heaven. We get to live here on earth for a while then live in heaven forever. Death isn't such a hard thing to think about after all, is it?

Sermon Ending:

I brought each of you a key today as a reminder that Jesus holds the key to the door into heaven. Don't lose site of the key to life, the key to death, the key to heaven — Jesus.

Devotional Ending:

(Presenter should hold up a key.) Remember that Jesus holds the key to the door into heaven. Don't lose sight of the key to life, the key to death, the key to heaven — Jesus.

Prayer:

Now, bow your head, close your eyes, and let's talk to God. You say after me: **"Dear God, Thank you for giving me life on earth and in heaven. Thank you for Jesus. Amen."**

(The best keys to use or the plastic ones that come on rings for babies. They are large and colorful. I found sets with 4 or 5 on a ring at Dollar Tree. The sets come apart so you can give each child one key.)

#6
Which Way?
Based on Psalms 25:8-10

THEME: Let God be your compass.

Have you ever been told not to do something, but you did it anyway? *(Presenter may want to substitute a personal story here. This was a true story about my son.)* There was a little boy by the name of Luke who was turning three years old, and his mother was planning a birthday party for him. All of his grandparents, aunts, uncles, and cousins were coming, and his mother made this very special chocolate birthday cake for him. She spent a long time just decorating the cake because she wanted everything to be just right. Now, you have to understand that Luke loved chocolate, and his mom could see in his eyes that he wanted some of that cake before everybody came for the party. He didn't want to wait. So his mother said, "Luke, stay out of the cake. You have to wait for the party. Promise me." He said, "Okay."

The mother went to her bedroom to change clothes and when she came out, she saw Luke's stool in front of the cabinet where his birthday cake was. Across the top of the cake were four little stripes where four little fingers had raked across it.

The mother found Luke in his room with chocolate smeared all over his face. He looked at her very seriously and said, "Daddy did it!"

Sometimes we are so tempted by people or things that we lose our direction. We know right from wrong, but it's hard to stay on the right path. You can end up doing the wrong thing even if you are just two or three years old. That's because doing the wrong thing can be more fun sometimes.

(Presenter needs to show a road map here.) Knowing the right direction to take in a car is not so hard because we have maps to show us how to get where we are going. If you are out in the woods, you can figure out which direction to go by using a compass. *(Show a compass here.)* A compass always points in the same direction and helps you stay on the right path. But knowing which direction to take in life, doing the right thing when the wrong thing would be more fun, requires help from God. We have to look to God to be our compass.

Bible Verse:

Our Bible verse today comes from **Psalms 25:10.** You say after me: **"When we obey God, every path he guides us on is fragrant with his loving kindness and his truth."**

You know that little feeling you get when you do something wrong, and you know it's wrong before you do it? That's God talking to you. He's saying, "You are headed in the wrong direction. You need to turn around."

Sermon Ending:

To help you remember our lesson today, I brought each of you a compass. Remember that God is the compass of your heart.

Devotional Ending:

Always remember that God is your life's road map. He is the

compass of your heart.

Prayer:

Now, bow your head, close your eyes, and let's talk to God. You say after me: **"Dear God, Lead me in the right direction. Help me to always choose what is right. Amen."**

(Plastic compass watches can be found in packets for birthday party favors, or you can order plastic compasses through the Oriental Trading Catalog *by the gross for less than $10. 00. You could also substitute a small copy of any road map and say that God is the road map of your heart. Small maps can be printed from your computer from travel internet sites.)*

#7
The Gift Of Grace
Based on Ephesians 1:7-8

THEME: God gives you the gift of forgiveness — grace.

(Presenter will need to have a small wrapped present.) What is this? It's a present. We know it is a present because it is wrapped in pretty paper and has a bow on it. The wrapping is to cover up what is inside until it is time for it to be opened.

When someone gives you a present, it is not because they have to, it is because they want to. It's a gift. A gift means that it is free. You don't have to buy it or work for it. You just have to accept it. And it is always a good idea to thank whoever gives it to you.

God's grace is like a present. GRACE. Say that word for me. GRACE. Grace is something God gives you that you can't buy or work hard enough for — something you can't be or act good enough to deserve. It is a gift — free. All you have to do to receive it is to accept it and believe that Jesus is your Lord and Savior.

Some of you may be wondering what grace is. Well, grace

can mean a lot of things, but the kind of grace you get from God is forgiveness — forgiveness for anything and everything you do wrong. Do you know who bought the gift of grace for you? Jesus did. When he died on the cross, his blood bought you God's grace. Then Jesus rose from the dead to be your Lord and Savior. Believing that and accepting that is the way you receive God's grace.

Bible Verse:

The Bible verse today comes from **Ephesians 1:7-8**. You say after me: **"God took away all our sins through the blood of his son, by whom we are saved; and has showered down upon us the richness of his grace."**

This wrapping paper covers up a gift inside. All you have to do to receive it is to accept it and open it. Think of grace as being a present. All you have to do to receive it, is accept it and open up to Jesus.

Sermon Ending:

I brought each of you a present today, but I want you to wait until in the morning to open it. When you do open it, I hope that it will remind you that God gives you a present every single morning — the gift of forgiveness — grace. And remember to thank him for that.

Devotional Ending:

God gives you a present every single morning — the gift of forgiveness — grace. Remember to thank him for that.

Prayer:

Now, bow your head, close your eyes, and let's talk to God. You say after me: **"Dear God, Thank you for the gift of grace. Thank you for Jesus. Amen."**

(I made each child a bracelet using leather and those beads with a letter on them. I used the letter beads W, W, J, and D for the saying: "What would Jesus do?" You can buy those beads and leather strips at any craft store like Michael's or Hobby Lobby. You, of course,

could put anything in the present that you wish, but it needs to be something the child would want to keep since it is representing God's gift of grace. You can buy gift boxes at the craft stores, but they, along with bows, are cheaper at dollar stores like Dollar Tree. Each package should be the same size as the others so the children will know they are all getting the same thing.)

#8
Things Change
Based on Psalms 59:10

THEME: In an ever-changing world, God is a constant.

I brought a kaleidoscope with me today. I am going to pass it around so that everyone can look through it. When you turn this piece, it makes different designs. The patterns change every time you turn it.

One of the things in life you can be sure of is change. Things change. People change. Listen to the sound of that word: C-H-A-N-G-E. Say it with me: CHANGE. Each one of you has changed a lot over the last year. You don't look the same as you did a year ago. You don't act the same.

Things around you change too. The weather often changes from one day to the next. The seasons change the world around us. In summer it is hot; in the autumn the weather begins to cool off, and the trees turn beautiful colors before their leaves fall, leaving them bare for winter. Then, in the spring, the leaves come back, and there are flowers everywhere.

Sometimes changes in our lives are good, and sometimes they are bad. A good change might be getting to move into a brand-new house. A bad change might be the illness or even death of someone you love.

As long as you live, everything and everyone around you will change from one day to the next, sort of like my kaleidoscope. But there is one thing that will never change, and that is the word of God, the Bible. The Bible tells us how to deal with changes that will affect us as we go through this life. The Bible teaches us that God is constant; he does not change. We can count on God to be with us, and be sure that no matter what happens to us on this earth, God will love us and bring us to heaven with him when the time is right, if we believe in his word.

In an ever-changing world, God is a constant. He is our rock. He is our foundation.

Bible Verse:

The Bible verse today comes from **Psalms 59:10**. You say after me: "**My God is changeless in his love for me, and he will come and help me.**"

Sermon Ending:

I brought each of you a little kaleidoscope today to remind you that in our ever-changing world, God's word and God's love for us will not change.

Devotional Ending:

The next time something changes in your life, remember my kaleidoscope, and try to understand that the world we live in is ever-changing, but God's word and God's love for us will not change. That is our constant.

Prayer:

Now, bow your head, close your eyes, and let's talk to God. You say after me: "**Dear God, Help us deal with the changes in our lives. Thank you for the Bible and your love. Amen.**"

(I bought kaleidoscopes, 3 to a package at Dollar Tree. However, I have since found religious kaleidoscopes in the Oriental Trading Catalog. *They are great.)*

#9

The Rainbow — The Promise
Based on Genesis 6:14 and 9:8-17

THEME: Be a pleasure to God.

Back when God created the first man and woman, Adam and Eve, he let people live for a very long time. They got really old, probably because God wanted them to have time to have lots of children so that the world would fill up with people. Well, the people who were born started acting ugly as they grew up, and their children acted ugly, and their children acted ugly. After awhile God looked down on the earth at all the sin and ugliness of the people, and the Bible says it broke God's heart.

God found only one family that still loved him and worshiped him. That was Noah's family. The Bible says that Noah was a pleasure to God.

God's patience with the sinful people finally ran out, and he told Noah to build a boat - a very big boat - big enough to hold Noah's family and two of every kind of animal on earth. Think about it. That was quite a big order, but Noah did what God told him to do, exactly the way God told him to do it.

The boat was called an ark, and after it was finished, God sent torrential rain for forty days and nights, and every thing on earth died except for Noah's family and the animals on the ark. They had to stay on that boat for a year before it was dry enough for them to come out and live. Noah had a lot of patience, didn't he? You see, he trusted God to know what was right for him and his family.

Because Noah was faithful to God, God promised that he would never again destroy the world with water. God said, "I seal this with a promise until the end of time, to you and to all the earth." And do you know what God's sign was and still is to this day? **A rainbow!**

Like Noah, we live in a world full of people who act ugly and who don't know God, and we can either join in and act ugly with them, or we can act the way God wants us to, perhaps influencing others to act the right way.

Bible Verse:

The Bible verse today comes from **Genesis 6:14**. You say after me: **"Noah was a pleasure to the Lord."**

We aren't perfect, but we can follow Noah's example and be a pleasure to God even if others around us are acting ugly.

Sermon Ending:

I brought each of you some crayons today and a picture of a rainbow over Noah's ark to color. Remember God's promise to Noah and to us. The next time you see a rainbow — GET EXCITED ABOUT IT! That's God talking to you!

Devotional Ending:

Remember God's promise to Noah and to us. The next time you see a rainbow, GET EXCITED ABOUT IT! That's God talking to you!

Prayer:

Now, bow your head, close your eyes, and let's talk to God. You say after me: **"Dear God, Thank you for your promises.**

Help us to deserve them. Amen."

("Noah and the Ark" pictures are usually found in Bible story coloring books. I asked one of my students to draw a picture for me and got his permission to xerox it. It looks nicer if you mount the picture on a piece of construction paper. The crayons can be purchased at dollar stores, several boxes per packet, or from the Oriental Trading Catalog.*)*

#10
Is Your Conscience Clear?
Based on Luke 16:13

THEME: Make God the master of your conscience.

I want you to meet someone today. The someone I want you to meet always knows right from wrong and is very honest. This someone can talk to you, but you can't actually hear their voice with your ears. This someone can keep you out of trouble if you listen. If you let this someone guide you, you may not always come out on top of things. In fact, you may end up with less money, you may lose if you are playing a game, and you may not always have as much fun if you follow this someone's advice, but *you will be a winner in life.*

The someone I want you to meet is your conscience. Did you know you even had one of those? Well, you do. Your conscience comes out when you want to do something you are not supposed to do. It is that little voice inside you that says, "You know you are not supposed to do that. Don't do it! Don't do it!"

Every time you listen to your conscience, it becomes stronger and healthier and clearer, and you become a stronger and happier person. But if you ignore your conscience, it will become cloudy and unhealthy, and before you know it, you will no longer be able to hear or feel your conscience at all.

Bible Verse:

The Bible verse today comes from **Luke 16:13**. You say after me: **"For neither you nor anyone else can serve two masters."**

That means either you are an honest person or you're not, either you are trustworthy or you're not, either you serve God or you don't. There is an old saying, "Let your conscience be your guide." Well, a clear and healthy conscience will keep you from cheating. A clear conscience will keep you from lying. A clear conscience will keep you from hurting others on purpose. A clear and healthy conscience will help you realize what is truly important in life. Keep your conscience clear and healthy by serving God.

Sermon Ending:

I made each of you a cloudy mirror today. *(Pass them out here.)* Hold your mirror close to your face. You can barely see your reflection, can you? A cloudy mirror is sort of like a cloudy conscience. You see, your conscience is a reflection of your master. If your master is money or stuff or drugs or the devil, then your conscience will become as hard to see as your face in a cloudy mirror. But if your master is God, then your conscience will be as clear as your reflection in a real mirror. I want you to look into your cloudy mirror in the mornings when you wake up, and then look into a good mirror. Let that help you to decide each and every day to make God the master of your conscience so that you will be able to see clearly the difference between right and wrong.

Devotional Ending:

When you get home, ask for a piece of aluminum foil about the size of a sheet of paper, and then hold it up close to your face like a mirror. You will see your reflection, but it will be cloudy. A cloudy mirror is sort of like a cloudy conscience. You see, your conscience is a reflection of your master. If your master is money or stuff or drugs or the devil, then your conscience will become as hard to see as your face in a cloudy mirror. But if your master is God, then you conscience will be as clear as your reflection in a real mirror. Decide each and every day to make God the master of your conscience so that you will be able to see clearly the difference between right and wrong.

Prayer:

Now, bow your head, close your eyes, and let's talk to God. You say after me: **"Dear God, Keep my conscience clear and healthy. Help me see your reflection in me. Amen."**

(I made the cloudy mirrors using cardboard that I had saved out of packs of paper, or you could use poster board or card stock. I covered one side with aluminum foil and the other side with a colorful sheet of computer stationary. I added some butterfly stickers to the foil side to make it more decorative.)

#11
Feed My Sheep, Little Lambs
Based on John 21:15-17

THEME: A little kindness goes a long way.

Would you sing a song with me today? I want us to sing *"Jesus Loves Me."* Everybody sing with us.

Jesus loves me this I know
For the Bible tells me so
Little ones to him belong
They are weak but he is strong.
Yes, Jesus loves me
Yes, Jesus loves me
Yes, Jesus love me
The Bible tells me so.

Thank you. That was beautiful. That song tells us that Jesus loves us. Now, let me ask you a question. Do you love Jesus? Jesus asked one of his disciples, Simon Peter, three times if he loved him. Each time Simon Peter said, "Yes, of course I do." And do you know what Jesus said back to him? He said, "If you love me, then feed my sheep."

I don't think Jesus was talking about feeding a flock of woolly little lambs. I think Jesus was talking about helping people. Jesus wanted Simon Peter to serve him and love him by loving and serving others and telling others about him.

There is something I have noticed about Jesus. When he asks us to serve him, it is always about us doing for others. Jesus is all about *love* and *kindness* and *sharing* and *giving* and *helping* others. Wouldn't the world be something if everybody had the same motives, the same reasons as Jesus Christ? Being a Christian means being a follower of Christ. The world would be a lot better if just all the Christians had the same motives as Jesus Christ.

Did you know that each one of you can make a difference in our world? I don't mean when you are grown. I mean now. You can change the world by loving and helping others. When you do that, you are feeding Jesus' sheep. When you do that, you are being Christ-like. When you do that for Jesus, you are being a Christian.

Bible Verse:

The Bible verse today comes from **John 21:16**. You say after me: **"'Take care of my sheep,' Jesus said."**

A little kindness goes a long way. *(Point to different children as you say the following.)* If you and you and you and you show kindness to others, and then they show kindness and then they show kindness and so on ... then you have changed the world. It can all begin with you.

Sermon Ending:

I made each of you a little lamb magnet to put on your refrigerator. Every time you go into your refrigerator to get something to eat, remember what Jesus said — "If you love me, feed my sheep."

Devotional Ending

I want to give you an assignment for this week. Every time you go into your refrigerator to get something to eat, I want you

to remember what Jesus said — "If you love me, feed my sheep."
Prayer:

Now, bow your head, close your eyes, and let's talk to God. You say after me: **"Dear God, Help me to be Christ-like. Help me to love Jesus by loving and serving others. Amen."**

Go forth and change the world little lambs!

(I made the lamb magnets using the pattern in the book "Bible Fun for Everyone." My introduction will tell you how to get the book. You can find small magnet squares on adhesive strips in the craft section of Walmart or most hobby or craft stores.)

#12
Handy Hands
Based on Luke 10:27-35
(a "Good Samaritan" story)

THEME: Use your hands wisely; use them to please God.

    I want you to hold out your hands, and take a good look at them. Have you ever thought about how really neat it is to have hands? Think what all you can do with them. You can use them to eat with, you use them to turn on a light in the dark, to open doors, and to pick up your favorite toy. I like it when someone I love holds my hand. It makes me feel loved and safe.

    You can use your hands to play musical instruments. Aren't we all glad that our church organist has hands? His hands make our church services so special. Let's clap our hands for him. Other people's hands affect you and your hands affect other people.

    Listen to this story about a teacher and a couple of her students. This teacher taught school in a prison. She put numbers on her pencils and assigned them to her students as a way to keep up with them better. She had two classes that used them. A prisoner in her second class who was assigned pencil #20 got very angry one day because pencil #20 had been chewed on around the lead. *(Presenter should have an ordinary yellow pencil with a white strip taped around the top. #20 needs to be written on the strip.)* He said, "When I find out who that idiot is that has been eating on my pencil, I'll give him something to gnaw on. I'll let him gnaw on my fist." The teacher gave him a new pencil and managed to calm him down. She said to her student, "For heaven's sake, don't let a pencil steal your joy."

The next morning the teacher realized who was assigned pencil #20 in her first class. It was a new student who had only one hand and arm. You see, he couldn't sharpen the pencil so he chewed the wood off around the lead so he could finish his lessons. He didn't want to ask anyone to sharpen it for him.

Often times people need help, and they won't ask for it. It can be a little thing like sharpening a pencil. The deal is, we need to take notice of others around us and reach out to help them if we can, and give them a hand.

You have heard the story about the good Samaritan from the Bible, where a Jewish man was beaten and robbed and left to die. A couple of normally good Jewish people saw him and passed him by. They didn't want to bother with him. Finally, a Samaritan came by. Samaritans were despised by the Jews. Jews didn't like them, and they sure didn't want them for neighbors. But out of the three people who came by, it was the Samaritan, the man of a different kind, a different race, who stopped and took the time to give help to another human being. He was a good neighbor.

Bible Verse:

The Bible verse today comes from **Luke 10:27**. You say after me: "**. . . Love your neighbor just as much as you love yourself.**"

You have been blessed with hands. They are these incredible tools that can change bad into good, meanness into kindness, sadness into happiness, hate into love — depending on what you do with them. Use your hands wisely. Use them to please God.

Sermon Ending:

To help you remember our lesson today, I brought each of you some clapping hands. We clap our hands to show someone we like what they did. Remember that God really likes it when you use your hands to bless others.

Optional Sermon Ending:

To help you remember our lesson today, I brought each of you a pencil with #20 taped around it. Let it remind you that sometimes people need help and won't ask for it. Be aware of others around you, and give them a helping hand.

Devotional Ending:

Sometimes people need help and won't ask for it. Be aware of others around you, and give them a helping hand.

Prayer:

Today, let's hold hands while we pray. Bow your head, close your eyes, and you say after me: **"Dear God, Thank you for my hands. Bless them so that I might use them to help others and be a good neighbor. Amen."**

(I found the little hand clappers at Dollar Tree in the party favors section. However, if you can't find them there, the Oriental Trading Catalog *has them. If you choose the optional ending, just use regular yellow school pencils.)*

#13
Spread A Little Sunshine
Based on Matthew 5:38-48
(loving your enemies)

THEME: Share you Christian joy with your friends and your enemies.

Our lesson today is about loving your enemies. The dictionary defines an enemy as someone who hates you or someone who wants to hurt you or someone who doesn't want to get along with you at all. Enemy is a strong word, isn't it?

Let me tell you what Jesus says about enemies. He says to love your enemies. Do good to those who hate you, pray for those who talk ugly to you and about you, and he says to ask God's blessing on those who hurt you. WOW! That is a very tall order. In fact, it might be one of the hardest things we ever do, but Jesus gives us a good idea on how to get started. He says, "Treat others as you want them to treat you." I've noticed that when I do that, things often change. The other person softens up and starts acting nicer towards me. However, if I'm ugly to an enemy, it just makes them dislike me more, and what good does that do either one of us?

It's hard to go through life without making some enemies along the way. Sometimes it happens and it not even be your fault. Someone might dislike you because you are a better ball player than they are. You could make an enemy simply because you are pretty or have more money, or perhaps you can sing better or play the piano. Maybe you make better grades in school. If that happens, I don't think Jesus would want you to quit playing ball or stop singing or flunk out of school. Jesus wants you to treat that enemy with kindness, pray for him or her to have a change of heart, and then for you to be the best person you can be. He wants you to be a Christian.

Jesus said that God gives his sunlight to both the evil and the good. That is a good example for us. We need to spread a little sunshine to those who love us and to those who don't.

Bible Verse:

The Bible verse today comes from **Matthew 5:44**. You say after me: "**Love your enemies! Pray for those who hurt you.**"

If you do good only to those who do you good, is that so wonderful? The Bible says even sinners and scoundrels do that. Follow God's example and spread your sunshine to everyone. It will make your world — the whole world — a brighter place.

Sermon Ending:

I made each of you a sunshine cookie today. Let it remind you to spread a little sunshine. Share your Christian love and your Christian joy with your friends and your enemies.

Devotional Ending:

Share your Christian love and your Christian joy with your friends and your enemies.

Prayer:

Now, bow your head, close your eyes, and let's talk to God. You say after me: "**Dear God, Give me the ability to love my enemies. Help me to spread love and joy everyday. Amen.**"

Goldfish and Silver Kisses

(I made large round sugar cookies and iced them with bright yellow frosting. I put candy corn around the edges. The frosting recipe on the back of the powdered sugar box works well because it hardens enough that they won't get smudged in the individual zip-lock bags.)

#14
Lost And Found
Based on Luke 15:11-24, 32
(the prodigal son)

THEME: The difference between bitterness and joy is our being able to forgive.

(This is a story about my own dogs, but I have written it in third person for you to tell. If you cannot find a picture of an Afghan hound, you could easily substitute the breed of dog. Calendar pictures are good to use because they are so large. You may want to tell this story using your own dogs and their names, if you have any dogs.) I want to tell you a story about two dogs. Tristin is an Afghan hound and looks like this, *(show a picture)* and the other one is a beagle named Pfister. This is a picture of him. Pfister is a little bit jealous of Tristin for several reasons. You see, Tristin is tall and can run very, very fast, and he can jump really high. Tristin has a bark that is so loud and so deep that it makes him sound ferocious and important. Tristin is so quick that when he chases something, he can catch it, which was a big surprise to the neighbor's cat. One day the dogs' owner, Linda, opened the gate to get

Goldfish and Silver Kisses

some firewood, and Tristin took that opportunity to escape the back yard. He ran like the wind, and before Linda knew it, he was out of sight. Linda grabbed her keys and set out to look for Tristin. He was finally found by a state trooper, miles from home chasing someone's cows. Thankfully, those cows didn't end up like the neighbor's cat. Linda was so glad to see Tristin that she hugged that dog and kissed him and brushed him and made him a bacon cheeseburger.

Pfister, on the other hand, wasn't feeling the same way Linda was. What he saw was Tristin being rewarded for running away. Pfister had not even tried to run off. He had acted the way he was supposed to, yet Tristin was getting all this special treatment for doing the wrong thing. Pfister threw his head back and howled and cried as though he was the most mistreated dog in Texas. He couldn't enjoy his bacon cheeseburger for feeling so bitter towards Tristin.

The difference between bitterness and joy is our being able to forgive. Pfister couldn't enjoy Tristin's homecoming because he was bitter and jealous. God doesn't want us to be that way because God isn't that way. God forgives us when we make bad decisions, and he rejoices when we come back to him and try to do what is right. He forgives and so must we. Let God's forgiveness for us teach us to forgive others.

Bible Verse:

The Bible verse today comes from **Luke 15:32.** You say after me: **"It is right to celebrate, for your brother was lost and now is found."**

Sermon Ending:

I brought each of you some warm fuzzies today. When you get mad at someone, give them a warm fuzzy, and forgive them. You never know how important that may turn out to be.

Devotional Ending:

The next time you get mad at someone, forgive them. You

never know how important that may turn out to be.
Prayer:

Now, bow your head, close your eyes, and let's talk to God. You say after me: **"Dear God, Plant forgiveness in my heart. Keep me warm with the love it spreads. Amen."**

(The warm fuzzies were simply pom-poms like those used for stuffed animals' noses. I bought an assorted bag of 100 or more at Michael's, a craft store, then put 10 of assorted colors and sizes in a snack-sized zip-lock bag for each child. They are also available in the Oriental Trading Catalog.)

#15
God's Greatest Magic
Based on Mark 12:30-31

THEME: What you do with love will determine the course of your life.

I want to talk to you about the most important thing in the world. This thing is more valuable than a mountain of gold, but you can't sell it or buy it. It is more beautiful than diamonds and roses, but you can't really see it. It feels better than any other feeling, yet you can't really touch it. This thing is the most powerful force in the universe, and it is more gentle than a summer breeze. This thing I am talking about is LOVE.

Did you know that out of all God's rules, out of all his commandments, that the two most important ones are about love, and if you follow just those two, all the others would be covered? Jesus said they were the most important. The first one is "Love God with all your heart and soul and mind," and the second one is "You must love others as much as you love yourself." Jesus said no other commandments are greater than these. You see, those two rules sum up all God's laws.

Bible Verse:

Our Bible verses today were the ones I just told you from

Mark 12:30-31. I have put them together more simply. You say after me: **Love God and love others.**

Don't you think it is fantastic that God's greatest magic, the most powerful force in the universe, the stuff that rules our lives, can't be seen, it can't be touched, it can't be smelled, and it can't be heard? It can only be felt in your heart. And you know what? That is the way it is with Jesus. I have never seen Jesus. I have never touched him or smelled him or heard him speak, but I know he exists because I can feel him. I can feel him in my heart just as I can feel love.

When God gave us Jesus, he gave us an unending supply of his love, and what you do with that love will determine the course of your life. That is the magic of God.

Sermon Ending:

I brought each of you a magic wand today to help you remember that love is God's greatest magic. It is the magic that rules hearts. It is the magic that rules lives. It is the magic that rules the world. Remember God's most important rules: **Love God and love others.**

Devotional Ending:

Remember that love is God's greatest magic. It is the magic that rules hearts. It is the magic that rules lives. It is the magic that rules the world. Remember God's most important rules: **Love God and love others.**

Prayer:

Now, bow your head, close your eyes, and let's talk to God. You say after me: **"Dear God, Help me make the world a better place with the love you put in my heart. Amen."**

Go forth and spread a little magic!

(I found magic wands in an assortment of sparkling colors at Dollar Tree. There are also magic wands in the Oriental Trading Catalog. *Or, you could easily make your own with a pencil or some other type stick and glue a star on top. Glitter always adds a little magic.)*

#16
God's Rules — God's Rock
Based on Matthew 7:24-27

THEME: Rules are for our own good.

I want to talk to you about good choices and bad choices today. Our choices build our future. Listen to this story about a little girl and her choices.

There was a little girl named Anna Belle, and she loved to play outside. She had a swing set and a jungle gym; she even had a sandbox, but her favorite toy of the moment was a beach ball like this one. *(Presenter should have a beach ball to illustrate.)* She would practice throwing the ball up in the air and then try to catch it as it came down. She had gotten very good at it. This particular day she threw the ball way up in the air, and as she ran to catch it, she sneezed. ACHOOOO! *(Presenter should throw the ball out into the aisle.)* Her ball bounced on the sidewalk then rolled into the street.

Anna Belle knew the rules. She could play outside as long as she did not go past the cedar tree this side of the street. Anna Belle had a choice to make. She could choose to go and get her ball in the street, or she could mind the rules and wait until her mother could get it for her. Anna Belle ran inside to get her mother, but she had the phone in one hand, and she was cooking with the other.

What would Anna Belle choose to do? If she went out into the street and her mom saw her, she wouldn't get to play outside again for a long, long time, but if she left her ball in the street, it would surely get run over.

Everyone has choices to make everyday between doing the right thing or the wrong thing, and like Anna Belle, they often don't even see the most important thing between the choices. Anna Belle didn't stop to think why her parents said she must never go into the street. She figured out that her ball could get run over, but it didn't occur to her that she could get run over.

It's not hard to mind the rules when every thing is going smoothly; it is when something out of the ordinary happens, like when our ball rolls out into a busy street, that we find it hard to mind the rules.

God has rules about how we should live just like parents do, and they are for our own good. When we mind God's rules, it is like building a house on a solid rock. It will stand even when storms come around. When we don't mind God's rules, it is like building a house on the sand. When storms come up, the house will fall down.

Bible Verse:

The Bible verse today comes from **Matthew 7:24**. You say after me: **"All who listen to my rules and follow them are wise, like a man who builds his house on solid rock."**

Sermon Ending:

I brought you some rock candy to help you remember that your life will be sweeter if you build it on God's solid rock of rules, and one of his rules is minding your parents.

Devotional Ending:

Build your life on God's solid rock of rules, and one of his rules is to mind your parents.

Prayer:

Now, bow your head, close your eyes, and let's talk to God. You say after me: "**Dear God, Be my rock so I won't ruin my life on bad choices. Amen.**"

(Old fashioned rock candy, on a wooden stick, can be found in most candy stores. I found it individually wrapped at the World Market.)

#17
Don't Blame The Shepherd
Based on Psalm 23

THEME: If you walk with God, he will guide you all the way to heaven.

When a little boy named Luke was about three years old, he loved to eat orange-flavored ice cream Push-Ups. Sometimes his Mother would let him have one for a snack in the afternoon, but Luke started asking for two of them. His Mother told him she was afraid it would make his tummy hurt if he ate two of them and that one was plenty.

One day when Luke's Daddy picked him up from day care, Luke asked him if he would take him to the store and buy him two Push-Ups because one didn't fill him up any more. Luke's Daddy reminded him that Mom never let him have two Push-Ups because it might make him sick, however, Luke begged and pleaded until Daddy finally gave in.

The Father had to take Luke back to his office with him for a few minutes to finish up some work, and it wasn't long before Luke's tummy began to hurt. His Daddy took him straight home, and when they walked in the door, Luke said, "Mom, Daddy didn't mind you, and he made my tummy hurt!"

Children are not the only people who blame others for what they get themselves into. Grown-ups do it too. In fact, grown-ups sometimes blame God when we get ourselves into trouble.

There is a chapter in the Bible called *The Twenty-third Psalm*. That chapter tells us that God is our shepherd and like a shepherd, God will take care of us and give us what we need if we let him lead our lives. But often, we rebel against God, we don't mind his rules, and we find ourselves sick or hurt or sad. Too often we think we know how many "Push-Ups" we need and then we suffer the consequences.

Bible Verse:

The Bible verse today comes from **Psalm 23:1**. You say after me: **"Because the Lord is my shepherd, I have everything I need."**

God is perfect! That means he has never made a mistake. He made his perfect Commandments and rules out of love, not out of spite, and if you follow those rules, if you walk with God, he will guide you all the way to heaven, and you will live in the house of the Lord forever. That is his promise; that is his gift. That is your reward.

Sermon Ending:

I brought each of you a bookmark with *The Twenty-third Psalm* written on it. Ask someone to help you learn those verses, and then carry them in your heart. Whenever you find yourself sick or hurt or sad, ask God, your shepherd, for help, but for heaven's sake, don't blame the Shepherd.

Devotional Ending:

Find the *Twenty-third Psalm* in your Bible, and ask someone to help you learn those verses then carry them in your heart. Whenever you find yourself sick or hurt or sad, ask God, your shepherd, for help, but for heaven's sake, don't blame the

Shepherd.

Prayer:

Now, bow your head, close your eyes, and let's talk to God. You say after me: "**Dear God, Lead my life. Help me to not blame you or others when I don't follow the rules. Amen.**"

(Christian Book Stores have bookmarks and wallet cards with The Twenty-third Psalm *written on them. You could also make something like that on your computer.)*

#18

Figs, In-Deed!
Based on Luke 13:1-9

THEME: God wants us to be useful and to serve a purpose.

I want to talk to you about figs today. A fig is a type of fruit that grows on a tree. In the Bible there is a story Jesus told about a fig tree to teach a lesson about people. There was a man who planted a fig tree in his garden, and he went again and again to see if he could find any figs on it, but he was always disappointed. He waited for years for the tree to produce some figs, and when it didn't, he decided to have his gardener cut it down to make room for something that would produce some fruit. That useless fig tree was just taking up space and serving no purpose. Well, the patient gardener talked his boss into leaving the tree one more year and giving it another chance to make some figs, then if it didn't he would cut it down.

By telling this story, Jesus was trying to teach people that God plants us in his garden called Earth, and he loves us and cares for us and tends to us, but he expects something back in return. He wants us to be useful and serve a purpose — to do good works and deeds — not just take up space. He has even given us a special gardener, and his name is Jesus. Patient and loving Jesus has bought us more and more chances to get right with God, but in the end, if we don't decide to follow Jesus and seriously love God by being useful and serving his purpose in our lives, we will be like the barren fig tree that didn't produce any figs. We will be cut down, cut out of eternal life in heaven.

Bible Verse:

The Bible verse today comes from Luke 13:9. You say after me: **"If we get figs next year, fine; if not, I'll cut the fig tree down."**

Try to think of yourselves as being like the fig tree in that story, and try to think of your good deeds and love for God as being like figs. Every time you produce figs, good works or deeds, you please God. Jesus will be there to help you by tending your tree and making your figs even better. Jesus can turn your figs, your good deeds, into something special.

Sermon Ending:

I brought each of you a packet of Fig Newton cookies today to help you understand that you are like the fig tree meant to produce figs, except you are a person meant to produce good works and deeds for God. Your good deeds, with the help of Jesus, can become even more special, like when an ordinary fig is made into a delicious Fig Newton.

Devotional Ending:

(Presenter should hold up an individual-sized packet of Fig Newtons. They can be found in most grocery store check-out lanes.) You are like the fig tree meant to produce figs, except you are a person meant to produce good works and deeds for God. Your good deeds, with the help of Jesus, can become even more special, like when an ordinary fig is made into a delicious Fig Newton.

Prayer:

Now, bow you head, close your eyes, and let's talk to God. You say after me: **"Dear God, Help me to produce good works and deeds. Grant me the help of Jesus to make them special. Amen."**

(Individual packets of Fig Newton cookies can be bought in family size boxes for school lunches. Two large cookies are in each packet.)

#19
Debark
Based on Luke 19:1-10
(the Zacchaeus story)

THEME: Jesus can peel off ugly behavior.
    One of my favorite stories in the Bible is about a short little man and a sycamore tree. When I was growing up, we had a big sycamore tree in our front yard. It was great for climbing. Once I asked my grandmother, who knew almost everything, why the bark on our sycamore tree peeled off when I climbed up and down it. After scolding me for being a little girl/boy who liked to climb trees, she told me this story.
    She said: There was a short little man named Zacchaeus who had become very rich from cheating people. You see, he took up money from people for their taxes, but he made them pay more than they really owed, and he kept the extra for himself. No one liked him because of it.
    One day Jesus came to the town where Zacchaeus lived, and crowds of people came out to see him. Zacchaeus, being very short, couldn't see over the crowds, so he climbed up a sycamore

tree to get a glimpse of Jesus. As Jesus walked by, he called out to the little man by name, and that is what our Bible verse is about today.

Bible Verse:

The Bible verse comes from **Luke 19:5.** You say after me: **"Jesus said, 'Zacchaeus! Quick, come down! For I am going to be a guest in your house today.'"**

My grandmother told me that the reason the bark comes off the sycamore tree is because when Zacchaeus heard Jesus call him by name, he slid down that tree so fast that the bark peeled off, and sycamores have had peeling trunks ever since.

(The following is true and personal, so you may have to alter it to fit your lesson, or make the entire lesson read in third person.) The very first thing I did after my husband and I bought property to build a house on, was plant a sycamore tree in the front yard. It has gotten almost as big and beautiful as the one I climbed as a child. I no longer climb trees, but I often look at that one and remember my grandmother and the story of Zacchaeus, a man who stole money from his neighbors, a man people despised, who in one instant changed his heart and his life because Jesus called out to him. Instead of trying to hide what all he had done wrong, Zacchaeus opened up to Jesus and turned his wrongs into rights.

There were people who got mad at Jesus for going home with Zacchaeus that day because they didn't think Jesus should associate with a sinner like that. And that is why I love this story so. I figured out a long time ago that if Jesus could love and forgive a sinner like Zacchaeus, he could love and forgive a sinner like me.

Sermon Ending:

I brought each of you a leaf and a piece of bark from my sycamore tree to help you remember the story of Zacchaeus and how Jesus changed his heart. *(See notes below if you do not live in*

an area where sycamore trees grow.)
Devotional Ending:
Remember the story of Zacchaeus and how Jesus changed his heart. Let him have a go at yours.
Prayer:
Now, bow your head, close your eyes, and let's talk to God. You say after me: "**Dear God, Continue to peel off my ugly behavior, and leave me standing as smooth as the trunk of a sycamore tree. Amen.**"

(Sycamore bark is usually in strips and pieces on the ground beneath the tree. I picked nice full leaves off my tree and put one with a piece of bark in a gallon sized zip lock bag for each child. If you do not live in an area where sycamore trees grow, bless your heart, you could give each child a picture of Zacchaeus in the tree or simply a picture of a tree with a smooth trunk to color. Also, in the "Bible Fun For Everyone" craft book mentioned in the introduction, there is a very simple and cute project to make of Zaccheus and the tree.)

*Note:
Never underestimate the power of God or his influence on the children that he provides through you, his story teller. After this particular lesson about Zacchaeus and the sycamore tree, I had a parent tell me that they had to go that week and buy a sycamore tree to plant in their yard. Yes, the children really do listen!

#20
Armed With God's Trumpet
Based on Judges 6:1-7:25

THEME: Don't be surprised when God wants to use you.

Have any of you ever thought that you weren't old enough or big enough to be used by God? Perhaps you've thought you weren't smart enough or brave enough to be used by God. Well, I have a story for you that will change all that. It is a story about a little cowardly farmer named Gideon. Gideon lived in a land that had been taken over by some selfish, wicked people, the Midianites. The Midianites were so cruel that thousands of them rode on camels into the land where Gideon lived, destroyed all their crops, stole all their cattle and other livestock, stripped the land bare, and left those people, the Israelites, to starve. You see, Gideon and the rest of the people of Israel had been ignoring God for a long time, and it was only after their land was completely destroyed that they once again cried out to God for help.

God heard them, and he sent down an angel to talk to Gideon, of all people. The angel told Gideon that God wanted him to destroy the Midianites. Gideon, I think, either thought he was going crazy, or he was so scared that he asked the angel to have God prove that he really was talking to him — 3 TIMES! So God did what Gideon asked of him to prove that "Yes, I'm really talking to you, Gideon."

You know, God doesn't ask people to do something for him and then not help them, and he didn't do that to Gideon. God led Gideon to defeat the thousands of Midianites with only 300 men, and those men never lifted a sword. They lifted trumpets. God's angel told Gideon to have his men all blow their trumpets at the same time. *(Presenter should blow a horn here. See notes below on where to find paper trumpets.)* When they did, it frightened the Midianites so that they started killing each other!

Bible Verse:

The Bible verse today comes from **Judges 6:14.** You say after me: **"The Lord said to Gideon, 'Go with the strength you have and rescue Israel from the Midianites. I am sending you!'"**

Don't be surprised when God wants to use you. God changes what is wrong by using people like you to do what is right. God changes hatred by using people like you to teach others to love. God will arm you with what you need to fight his battles whether it is with words, actions, love, or the sound of a trumpet.

When we worship God, love God, and live for God, he arms us with the trumpet of Jesus, and friend, there is nothing more powerful on earth than the sound of that.

Sermon Ending:

I brought each of you a trumpet today to help you remember the story of Gideon, an unlikely hero, so that you will realize that God has a job for each of you, and he will give you what you need to accomplish it. (Let's all blow trumpets for God.) *(Allow children to blow them here so they won't be tempted during church. Also it creates quite an effect.)*

Devotional Ending:

Remember the story of Gideon, an unlikely hero, so you will grow up realizing that God has a job for you, and he will give you what you need to accomplish it.

Prayer:

Now, bow your head, close your eyes, and let's talk to God. You say after me: **"Dear God, With the spirit of Jesus, arm me with what I need to be your Christian soldier. Amen."**

(I used rolled paper horns that I found at a party store, 8 for $1.00. They were not the kind that extend when blown and curl up again. They resembled a cone and had a little mouth piece on the end. They were very loud when blown and more closely resembled the type Gideon would have used than anything else I came across. Card and party stores are great sources to find items for your church children. I stuck a sticker on each one to make them more attractive.)

#21
Daniel And Some Hungry Lions
Based on Daniel 6:1-28 and 7:4
(from the lions' point of view)

THEME: Talk to God everyday.

Do you know what my favorite food is? I love pizza! That delicious crust piled with meat and sauce and dripping with melted cheese. Now just imagine if I had not been allowed to eat for several days, and then all of a sudden someone handed me a piping hot pizza. Do you think I would want to eat it? Sure I would! I could eat some right this very minute. Just thinking about pizza this morning caused me to stop and order some on the way to church. In fact, it ought to be here just about now. Hi, *Sam.* Would you bring that down to us? *(I actually ordered pizza, had it delivered and brought up to the front of the church, and let the children go at it. Bring napkins! You'll need to talk to your local pizza place manager and set everything up a couple of days in advance. A reminder call never hurts. Also, you'll notice this lesson is longer than the others because the children will need time to eat their pizza. You might want to ask your pastor for a little more time for this service. I didn't tell mine why I needed it, and he was gracious enough not to ask. It's always more fun to surprise everybody, including the pastor.)*

Now that I have everybody in the church hungry for some of this hot, scrumptious, delicious pizza, I want to tell you a story about some hungry lions who didn't get to eat the food that was delivered to them — and a man named Daniel.

Daniel lived in Babylon where he worked for and advised King Darius. The king came to love and trust Daniel because Daniel was honest and wise. There were some other guys who also worked for the king, and they became jealous of Daniel because the king was planning to put Daniel in charge of them. So, they decided to get rid of Daniel. These guys knew how Daniel loved God and how he prayed to God everyday. They went to King Darius and talked him into making a new law saying that anyone who prayed to anyone other than the king would be thrown into the lions' den.

In the next day or two, those men went to Daniel's house and found him praying to God, just like they knew they would. King Darius was forced to have Daniel taken to the lions' den because Daniel disobeyed his new law. Since those men had been planning this, they made sure the lions hadn't been fed in awhile. Those lions were hungry, very hungry, and all of a sudden instead of someone delivering a pizza to them, they were given their favorite food — a living, breathing person!

Okay, now think about it. Those lions were hungry. They hadn't eaten in days, and all of a sudden this person is thrown to them for dinner. They can smell him. Their mouths start to water. Their stomachs began to growl, and they are ready to tear into him when <u>God stops everything</u>. He says to those lions, "Don't even think about it." The Bible says that God closed the lions' mouths where they couldn't eat Daniel. Don't you feel just a little sorry for those hungry lions?

You see, Daniel was faithful to God, and God was faithful to Daniel.

Bible Verse:

The Bible verse today comes from **Daniel 7:4**. You say after me: "**God does great miracles in heaven and earth. He delivered Daniel from the hungry lions.**"

Daniel was able to communicate with God because he made it a habit. He didn't wait to pray just when he needed something. He talked to God everyday, and God knew Daniel well.

Sermon Ending:

I made each of you a little lion out of Oreo cookies. God won't tell you not to eat the lion like he told the lions not to eat Daniel.

Devotional Ending:

Don't wait until you find yourself in big trouble to learn how to pray. Visit with God daily.

Prayer:

Now, bow you head, close your eyes, and let's talk to God. You say after me: "**Dear God, Give us the courage to obey you even in the face of danger. Amen.**"

(There are lots of children's illustrated books on Daniel and the lions' den. Use one to show pictures while telling the story. It will focus the children's attention to you while they are eating their pizza.)

("Oreo With a Twist" from the Better Your Home Series, *is where I found the lion cookie idea. I found the book in the check-out line at the grocery store. You could possibly order the book from **Meredith Integrated Marketing, Publishing Group of Meredith Corp., 1716 Locust St., Des Moines, IA 50309-3023**. You may not want to give another treat since they had the pizza, or you may want to give them some sort of lion treat of your choice and skip the pizza.)*

#22

Wrong Is Never Right
Based on Psalms 51:10

THEME: There isn't a right way to do the wrong thing.

Have you ever taken something that didn't belong to you? Have you ever pushed somebody because they cut in front of you or because they pushed you first? Have you ever told a lie about somebody because you didn't like them or because they told a lie about you? Have you ever told a lie about anything?

Most everyone grows up learning the difference between right and wrong. We learn it at home and at school and in church, but even though we all know right from wrong, we don't always choose right from wrong. The things we do wrong are called sins, and whenever we commit a sin against someone, we are committing a sin against God. Wow! When you think about it that way, it puts things in a different perspective. What that tells us is that when we steal something from someone, it is the same as stealing from God. If we push someone, it is the same as pushing God. When we lie or lie about someone, it is the same as lying about God.

We can make all the excuses we want as to why we sin and why we had a good reason to sin, but the truth is, there isn't a right way to do the wrong thing.

Bible Verse:

The Bible verse today comes from **Psalms 51:10.** You say after me: **"Create in me a pure heart, O God, and renew a steadfast spirit within me."**

I love the word *steadfast*. It means steady, firm, faithful, and loyal. Your parents, your teachers, and your church-house preachers can teach you right from wrong, but only God can create in you the desire to choose right from wrong.

When you sin, and we all do, tell God what you did wrong, ask him to forgive you, and ask him to give you the desire to not commit that sin again. Ask God to make you a steadfast Christian soldier.

In the military, soldiers wear dog tags like this. *(A member of your church or family will have a set of dog tags you can borrow if you don't have any of your own.)* They have the person's name, rank, birth date, blood type, and service number. In case something goes wrong and the soldier is killed or wounded, their dog tags identify them so there is no mistake as to who they are.

Sermon Ending:

I brought each of you some Christian dog tags to remind you that God knows your name, birth date, and blood type, and he has your number. You can't hide from him, and you can't hide your sins from him, but you can confess your sins, and he will help you choose right from wrong.

Devotional Ending:

God knows your name, birth date, and blood type, and he has your number. You can't hide from him, and you can't hide your sins from him, but you can confess your sins, and he will help you choose right from wrong.

Prayer:

Goldfish and Silver Kisses

Now, bow your head, close your eyes, and let's talk to God. You say after me: "**Dear God, Help me to be your steadfast Christian soldier so that I will choose right from wrong. Amen.**"

(Christian dog tags can be found in the Oriental Trading Catalog.*)*

#23

Give What You Are
Based on Matthew 19:16-22 and I Timothy 6:18

THEME: Hold on to innocence, faith, and love, but give what you are.

There is a story in the Bible about a rich young man who was alive when Jesus was still on earth. This young man went to Jesus one day and asked him what to do to have life in heaven. Jesus told him he needed to mind The Commandments. The man told Jesus that he always obeyed The Commandments. Then Jesus looked at him and said, "If you want to be perfect, go and sell everything you have and give the money to the poor, and you will have treasures in heaven." The young man went away sadly because he was very rich, and he didn't want to give away everything.

Jesus didn't tell everybody to do that. Perhaps he looked into that rich man's heart and saw that money was what he was about, money was who he was. I think Jesus could see that the young man loved money more than he loved people or God. God wants us to be able to support ourselves. A person doesn't have to be poor and homeless to be a Christian. God just wants us to gladly share what we have with him by sharing with others who are in need. He doesn't want us to love money or things more than we love other people or him.

There are many things we can give to people as well as money. We can give our help, our knowledge, our know-how, share our experiences, and lend a shoulder for someone to cry on. We can give our time; we can give our love. We not only need to give what we have, we need to give what we are.

Bible Verse:

The Bible verse today comes from **I Timothy 6:18**. You say after me: **"Use your money to do good. Be rich in good works and give happily to those in need."**

When Jesus looked into the heart of that young rich man, he saw what that man loved the most. Perhaps he could see that money and riches were keeping that man from finding true joy and real love. When Jesus looks inside the heart of a child, he usually finds innocence, faith, and love, but as we grow up, often we allow those things to become dark with worry, responsibility, hard times, and even rich times.

Sermon Ending:

I brought each of you a chocolate light bulb today. It is to encourage you to hold on to the innocence, faith, and love that lights up your heart right now. That is the light that allows you to give what you are.

Devotional Ending:

Hold on to the innocence, faith, and love that lights up your heart right now. That is the light that allows you to give what you are.

Prayer:

Now, bow your head, close your eyes, and let's talk to God. You say after me: **"Dear God, Keep my heart burning bright with love, faith, and innocence. Help me to give what I am.**

Amen."

(I found the chocolate light bulbs at The World Market. The Oriental Trading Catalog has several glow-in-the-dark items, plastic flashlights, and even some plastic magic bulbs that light up when touched. Anything that gives light would work fine.)

#24
Jesus, Be My Umbrella
Based on Matthew 4:1-10

THEME: Jesus can protect you from temptation.

Did you know that God is a master teacher? He knows how to teach each one of us lessons about life in the very way we will learn the best and the most. Not only is God your best teacher and my best teacher, he was Jesus' best teacher.

You see, God wanted to teach Jesus how to have real understanding for people. He could have said, *"Son, people will face hunger and poverty. They will be tempted by things they want. Others will seek power while some will have problems with pride; you know, wanting to show off to others. So, Jesus, I want you to realize all this and be sympathetic for them when they face these problems; understand how they feel."* But God, in his wisdom, knew the best way to learn and understand something is by sometimes going through it.

After Jesus was baptized, God had the Holy Spirit lead Jesus into the wilderness, and he left him there for forty days and nights with no food! Do you think Jesus learned what it felt like to be hungry? Sure he did! But if that wasn't enough, God allowed Satan to get to Jesus. Satan, the devil, tried to tempt hungry Jesus into turning the rocks around him into loaves of bread. Jesus had the power to do it, but he knew that wasn't what God wanted him to do.

Then the devil took Jesus to the roof of a temple and tried to persuade him to jump off so that the others would see angels come and protect him from the fall, proving to them that he really was the Son of God, but Jesus knew better than to test God.

Next, the devil told Jesus he would give him the world and everything in it if he would just kneel down and worship him, but Jesus, as hungry and poor and weak as he was, said "No!" to the devil and told him to leave.

Through those trials and temptations, through the hunger and the poverty, God taught Jesus self-discipline, patience, trust, and faith — not from a Godly point of view but from a human point of view.

People are tempted everyday to do the wrong things, and the devil is right there with us pushing us to make the wrong choices, but guess who else is there. Jesus is, and he truly understands how hard it is to always do the right thing. With that understanding he can help us see that following God and doing what is right is the only choice.

Bible Verse:

The Bible verse today comes from **Matthew 4:10**. You say after me: **"'Get out of here, Satan,' Jesus told him."**

Think of Jesus as being like your umbrella and the devil like a hard rain. *(Presenter should open an umbrella here.)* An umbrella won't stop the rain from falling, but it will keep you from getting all wet.

Sermon Ending:

I brought each of you a tiny umbrella today to help you remember that Jesus will help keep the devil off you.

Devotional Ending:
The next time you are under an umbrella, think of Jesus. Think about how he can protect you from the devil — if you will only let him.

Prayer:
Now, bow your head, close your eyes, and let's talk to God. You say after me: "**Dear God, I want Jesus to be my umbrella and protect me from the devil's rain of temptations. Amen.**"

(Paper umbrellas used in tropical drinks are available in the Oriental Trading Catalog as well as real-size paper ones on a bamboo handle. World Market has them too. The umbrella I used to open during the lesson was a paper one on a bamboo handle. It made a great effect.)

#25
We Come In Different Flavors
Based on John 13:34

THEME: No matter our color on the outside, we're all the same color on the inside.

Have you ever thought about all the different flavors there are? There are chocolate, vanilla, strawberry, lemon, cinnamon, orange, caramel, and many others. What would life be like if there was only vanilla? There would be no more chocolate cake, no more orange juice or lemonade, and no more strawberry jelly. Things would start to taste very boring.

What if all people were just alike? That would be boring too. That is one reason why God made people in so many flavors. There are Mexicans, Africans, Caucasians, Indians, Arabs, Italians, and Chinese just to name a few, and all of them have different colors of skin. Not only that, they have their own culture as well. That means they have there own special way of life.

For example, they have their own languages, special foods unique to them, and they even have clothes and jewelry that we can recognize as being from a particular culture.

Goldfish and Silver Kisses

One of the reasons we are so lucky to live in America is that there are lots of different flavors of people who live here from all over the world. It is one of the things that makes our country so great. You see, we learn from each other. Our differences have made our nation stronger.

Optional: *If you live in a country other than the United States of America, you can substitute the name of your country or continent. For example, if you live in Europe, you might say, "One of the reasons we are so lucky to live in Europe is because there are so many nationalities of people who live around us. It is one of the things that makes our country so great, etc.)*

The neat thing is that no matter what color we are on the outside, we are all the same color on the inside. God tells us to love one another no matter what color of skin a person is wrapped up in.

Bible Verse:

The Bible verse today comes from John 13:34. You say after me: **"Love each other just as much as I love you."**

Let's sing together the song *"Jesus Loves the Little Children."* (Everyone in the church join in.)

> *Jesus loves the little children*
> *All the children of the world*
> *Red and yellow, black and white*
> *They are precious in his sight*
> *Jesus loves the little children of the world.*

Sermon Ending:

To help you remember that God made people in different flavors, but that we are all the same color on the inside, I brought each of you a *Tootsie Roll Pop*.

Devotional Ending:

God loves variety, and that is why he made so many different races of people. Remember that all the races of the world are precious in God's sight, and he wants us to respect and value each

other's differences.
Prayer:
   Now, bow your head, close your eyes, and let's talk to God. You say after me: "**Dear God, Thank you for every flavor in the world. Thank you for how we are the same and for how we are different. Amen.**"

   (I stuck the different flavors of Tootsie Roll Pops in a plant and let the children pick the one they wanted. It was more interesting than just having them in a brown paper bag.)

#26
Nothing About Mad Feels Good
Based on Psalms 37:8-9

THEME: Ask God to replace your anger with peace.

Have you ever gotten mad? The next time you get mad, I want you to notice what happens to you. Your head will feel heavier, and you'll get this hot feeling that will start at your toes and move all the way up your body. When it reaches your head, you'll think it's going to explode! Oh, and you'll get this lump in your throat that you can't swallow because it attaches itself right above your Adam's apple so that you have to breathe hard or even cry.

When you think about it, nothing about mad feels good. So why do we do it? Why do we let ourselves get angry? Sometimes we just can't help it. Anger can grab hold of anybody. It is a human emotion that everyone comes equipped with. The thing is — getting mad is okay unless you stay that way. The Bible says to stop your anger, and turn off your wrath. Wrath is a heavier word for anger.

Instead of letting anger grow from your toes all the way up

to your head, ask God to make it disappear. Did you know that God will do that? If you stop for a minute and ask God to get rid of your anger, peace will replace it. Peace will gobble it up and make you feel better.

Bible Verse:

The Bible verse today comes from **Psalms 37:8-9.** You say after me: "**Stop your anger! Turn off your wrath! Don't fret and worry. It only leads to harm.**"

It's okay to get mad every once in a while, but it's not okay to stay that way. Get over it!

Sermon Ending:

I brought each of you some sidewalk chalk today. The next time you get mad, remember to take notice of how it feels. Then take your chalk, and draw a picture of whatever you are mad at on the sidewalk. Next, get a water hose or a bucket of water, and wash it away. That's sort of what God does when you ask him to get rid of your anger. He doesn't use a water hose, thank goodness. He washes away our anger with peace.

Devotional Ending:

The next time you get mad, remember to take notice of how it feels. On a piece of paper, draw a picture of whatever you are mad at. After you are done, take a good look at it, and then rip up the paper, and throw it away. After you have done that, ask God to rip away your anger and replace it with peace. God wants you to feel peace.

Prayer:

Now, bow your head, close your eyes, and let's talk to God. You say after me: "**Dear God, When anger starts growing in me, wash it away with your peace. Amen.**"

(*Sidewalk chalk is much larger than board chalk. You can buy it by the bucket at craft stores, Walmart, or the* Oriental Trading Catalog.*)*

#27
God's Traffic Rules — The Big Ten
Based on Exodus 20
(The Ten Commandments)

THEME: God expects us to try our best.

When you get old enough to drive a car, you are going to have to obey some traffic rules. You will have to drive on the right side of the road. You can't drive too fast or too slow. You'll have to use headlights in the dark. Seatbelts will be a must. You will have to stop at stop signs, pay attention to traffic lights, and no tailgating. If you don't follow these rules, patrolmen will stop you, tell you what you did wrong, and probably even write you a ticket. But those rules weren't made just so patrolmen could catch people being bad. Their purpose is to keep people safe.

God has some traffic rules. He calls his ***The Ten Commandments***, and like our traffic rules, they were made to help keep us safe and to steer us away from trouble.

• The first commandment says don't worship anybody but God.

• The next one says don't worship anything other than God.

- Another rule is to not talk ugly and especially to not use God's name in an ugly way.
- Also, we are supposed to keep the Sabbath day holy, and one way to do that is to go to church.
- The fifth commandment is to mind your mom and dad.
- Number six is that you must not murder people.
- The seventh commandment says that when you get married, you can't share romantic love with someone else's husband or wife.
- Number eight — don't steal.
- Number nine — don't lie.
- And the last one tells us not to wish that someone else's stuff belongs to us.

God doesn't drive a black and white patrol car with lights and sirens to make sure we follow his rules, and God doesn't write us tickets when we mess up. Just the same, God expects us to mind his rules for our own good as well as for the good of others. There are times you are going to mess up and break a rule and get into trouble because people aren't perfect. Just like sometimes really good people get traffic tickets. However, God expects us to try our best to be good and to follow his Ten commandments.

Bible Verse:

The Bible verse today comes from **Genesis 17:1**. You say after me: **"God said, 'I am the Almighty; obey me and live as you should.'"**

Sermon Ending:

I brought each of you a patrol car model that you can make at home. You might need some help with it. It's to remind you that God has traffic rules called *The Ten Commandments*, and like our highway traffic rules, they were made to keep us safe and help us know how to act.

Devotional Ending:

The next time you see a patrol car, I hope it will remind you of God's traffic rules called *The Ten Commandments,* and like our highway rules, they were made to keep us safe and help us know how to act.

Prayer:

Now, bow your head, close your eyes, and let's talk to God. You say after me: **"Dear God, Thank you for rules that keep me safe. Help me to follow them. Amen."**

(Some policing agencies, like DPS have cards with patrol cars printed on them. The children punch out the parts, fold at score lines, glue or tape the tabs, to create a model car. It is a project their parents or someone else could help with. If you cannot obtain something similar to that, you could always give them a little toy car. Packages of emergency vehicles can be found where toys are sold.)

#28
Life Has Its Ups And Downs
Based on James 1:2-3

THEME: Sometimes bad things turn out to be good things.

Have you ever had a really rotten, terrible, horrible, want-to-forget-about-it day? I'd like to tell you a story about a lady who had a really rotten, terrible, horrible, want-to-forget-about-it day. You see, on that particular day, a state trooper pulled this lady over for not wearing a seatbelt. She said, "Officer, I have had a really rotten, terrible, horrible, want-to-forget-about-it day. First, I overslept, and then my baby spit up all over my only clean dress, so I had to put on a dirty one. Then I went outside, and my car had a flat tire. I was late for work, of course, and my boss was angry about it. When lunch time came, I realized that I had left my purse at home and had no money to buy lunch, and now this!"

The state trooper said, "Ma'am, if you left your purse at home, does that mean you don't have your driver's license or proof of insurance with you?"

Well, that made her so mad that she started crying. She

Goldfish and Silver Kisses

shouted, "Yes, that's what it means! Just write me a ticket for everything, and while you're at it, include a ticket for a broken tail light. I forgot to mention that I backed into a telephone pole at work when I left."

The trooper gave her a ticket for no seat belt and a warning for everything else. When she drove off, she was so mad she could hardly see straight.

A few months went by and this very same trooper was in a café on his lunch break when that very same lady walked up to him and asked if she could give him a hug. She said, "I used to never wear my seatbelt until you stopped me and gave me a ticket for it. Two weeks after that ticket, I was in a bad car wreck. The paramedic told me that my seatbelt saved my life."

You see, what she thought had been a bad thing, turned out to be a very good thing. Sometimes God lets us have really rotten, terrible, horrible, want-to-forget-about-it days because he knows that it might change our wrong behavior into the right behavior. Also, we learn patience from the rough times we go through. It's a way of protecting us — sort of like a seatbelt.

Bible Verse:

The Bible verse today comes from **James 1:2-3**. You say after me: **"Be happy, for when the way is rough, your patience has a chance to grow."**

Sermon Ending:

To help you remember that life has its ups and downs, I brought each of you a yo-yo. Know that God loves you on "up" days and "down" days too.

Devotional Ending:

Every time you get into a car and buckle your seatbelt, think about God and how he can use our rotten, terrible, horrible, want-to-forget-about-it days for our own good.

Prayer:

Now, bow your head, close your eyes, and let's talk to God.

You say after me: "**Dear God, Help me to learn from my difficult days. Thank you for life's ups and downs. Amen.**"

(Yo-yos can be purchased in packages at dollar stores or can be ordered from the Oriental Trading Company Catalog *that is listed in the index. That catalog even has yo-yos with religious themes.)*

#29
Bless Others With A Smile
Based on Matthew 5:7

THEME: God wants us to bring joy to others.

I want for you to think of something that you almost always get back when you give it away. It's contagious and infectious but makes you feel better. It doesn't cost anything, but it's worth a lot. It means the same thing no matter what language you speak, and everybody understands it. What could that be? It's a SMILE!

Let's try an experiment. *(Presenter whispers to the children to face the congregation and give them their biggest and brightest smile, then see how many people smile back. If this is being done at home or somewhere else, ask the child to go about smiling to others in the household, grocery store, etc.)*

Wow! There's a lot of power in a smile, isn't there? You know, in I Chronicles 14:2, it says, "David realized why the Lord had made him king and why he had made his kingdom so great; it was for a special reason — to give joy to God's people."

We must remember that God placed us where we are and gave us all we have so we may bring joy and blessings to others

— not just to ourselves. One way to bless others is to give them a heart-warming smile and to show them kindness.

Bible Verse:

The Bible verse today comes from **Matthew 5:7**. You say after me: "**Happy are the kind and merciful, for they shall be shown mercy.**"

Sermon Ending:

When we are kind to others, it makes God smile. I know someone who smiles wherever he goes — even when traveling the roads on top of an antenna. His name is Mr. Box. Jack Box. You know, I can't help but smile when I see him. I brought each of you a Jack-in-the Box antenna ball. Perhaps he'll help you to remember to smile and bring some joy to others.

Devotional Ending:

When we are kind to others, it makes God smile. I know someone who smiles wherever he goes — even when traveling the roads on top of an antenna. His name is Mr. Box. Jack Box. I can't help but smile when I see him. The next time you see Jack Box on a car, SMILE, and let it be a reminder to smile more often and at more people. Bring joy to others.

Prayer:

Now, bow your head, close your eyes, and let's talk to God. You say after me: "**Dear God, Thank you for all the joy you have given me. Help me to bring joy to others. Amen.**"

(Actually, I was fortunate enough to work with someone whose daughter-in-law worked in the corporate end of Jack-in-the-Box. She brought me Jack-in-the-Box toys to give my church children. Wow! Thanks, Kelly and Lyndol.)

#30
Holy Ghost!
Based on Acts 2:1-13, Matthew 28:20

THEME: The Holy Ghost is the Spirit of God.

I want to talk to you about the Holy Spirit today. It is something hard to understand because we can't see it. Jesus is easier to understand because he actually came to earth. He was born as a human baby, lived and grew to be a man that talked and walked, slept, ate, and worked like a regular person. Of course Jesus was part of God, so he wasn't a regular person, and we found that out through the miracles he performed, and how he rose from the dead and came back to earth to teach people about the reason he came to earth to start with. But the Holy Spirit is harder to understand because the Holy Spirit is sort of like a ghost.

In fact, the Holy Spirit has been called the Holy Ghost because a ghost, like what we think of, is a spirit you can't see. The difference is we sometimes think of a ghost as being a dead person who haunts houses, or we pretend they fly around on Halloween night. But the Holy Ghost, the Holy Spirit, is very much alive. It is the Spirit of God. It doesn't haunt houses or fly around on Halloween. It comes to live inside living, breathing people. The Holy Spirit is the way through which God stayed on earth after Jesus went back to heaven.

When Jesus was on earth, he could only be in one place at one time, but through the Holy Spirit, Jesus can be all over everywhere at the same time. He can be inside me, inside you, inside millions of people anywhere in the world all at once. And if you ever decide to become an astronaut and travel into outer space, the Holy spirit can go there too.

Bible Verse:

The Bible verse today comes from **Matthew 28:20**. You say after me: "**Be sure of this, I am with you always, even to the end of the world.**"

Jesus said those words. He said them even though he knew he would not be walking around as a person and that he was going back to heaven. You see, when Jesus went back to heaven, he became one with God again. The Holy Spirit is the part of God and Jesus that stayed on earth so people would have access to them. That was a very smart way for God to handle that situation. Don't you think?

Sermon Ending:

I brought each of you something that resembles what we normally think of as a ghost, but it is really just a Kleenex draped over a lollipop. This ghost is pretend, but the Holy Ghost, the Holy Spirit, is very real. Believe in its power; it is the Spirit of God.

Devotional Ending:

The ghosts you see at Halloween time are pretend. They are fun to look at, but the Holy Ghost, the Holy Spirit, is very real and it is around all the time. Believe in its power; it is the Spirit of God.

Prayer:

Now, bow your head, close your eyes, and let's talk to God.

You say after me: "**Dear God, Thank you for leaving your spirit on earth so we can feel your presence. Amen.**"

(For the ghosts, I used Tootsie Roll Lollie Pops and put a white Kleenex over each one. I then tied a purple satin ribbon around each and tied it in a bow. I used a purple Sharpie marker to mark large eyes on the heads.)

#31
Does God Really Talk?
Based on Isaiah 58:9

THEME: God really does talk.
    All my life I have been taught to pray and that God answers prayer, but I have a confession to make. When I was your age, I had a hard time believing that God answered my prayers because I couldn't hear him speak. I would talk to God, but he wouldn't talk back. You see, I didn't understand how to listen. I have learned some things about God since then that I would like to share with you in this story.
    (This is a personal story that you could tell in third person or use a personal experience of your own.) A text-book company I sometimes work for asked me to go to Beaumont on a Saturday morning and give a workshop on one of their book series. I had to be there early that morning, so it was dark when I left Huntsville. The directions I had been given included several shortcuts, but it meant I would have to travel through little country towns and mostly just woods. I was nervous, and to make things worse, a fog had set in, and it was misting rain.

The farther I drove down those country roads, the heavier the fog got, and the more frightened I became. I could barely see the road in front of me, much less road signs showing me where to turn. I started talking out loud to God. I said, "God, you know how scared I am. Please help me." I wasn't expecting God to talk back, but something happened that dreary, foggy morning that I will never forget. I felt an angel on my shoulder. For a brief moment, a crisp flutter of air brushed my left shoulder and cheek, and a peace surrounded me that took my fear away. I knew without a doubt that God had sent me my guardian angel, even though the angel didn't speak.

A gas station store, just up the road, lit up the foggy darkness, and I pulled in and went inside. I looked around for a bit at the cookies and chips and soft drink cooler until the man behind the counter said sweetly, "Ma'am, the fog has lifted, you'll be alright now." I don't think that man knew that God was speaking through him.

Bible Verse:

The Bible verse today comes from Isaiah **58:9**. You say after me: **"Thou shalt call and the Lord shall answer and say, 'Here I am.'"**

God does answer prayer. God does talk back. You just have to learn to listen and recognize his voice.

Sermon Ending:

I brought each of you a bookmark with an angel pin — an angel for your shoulder to watch over you. This is only a symbol of the real angel that is already there.

Devotional Ending:

Each of you has an angel. The Bible says you do. Embrace your angel, and know that God is always with you.

Prayer:

Now, bow your head, close your eyes, and let's talk to God. You say after me: **"Dear God, Help me to recognize my angel** and your voice. Amen."

(The bookmarks with the angel pins are in the Oriental Trading Catalog *There are a number of angel items in the religious section to choose from.)*

#32

Answers On Board
Based on Luke 18:1-8 and Colossians 4:2

THEME: Learn to listen and watch for God's answers.

I want to tell you a story about a man named Barney. One day while listening to the news on TV, Barney heard the weatherman say a bad rainstorm was coming and that there was a good chance the whole area would be flooded. Barney wasn't worried because he would pray about it. He had faith that God would take care of him.

Sure enough, the rain began to fall, and it kept falling until the water started coming into Barney's house. Barney prayed, "God, save me from this flood." Well, it wasn't long before Barney heard some shouts outside. "Barney, we have come for you. Get into the canoe, and we will carry you to higher ground." Barney shouted back, "The good Lord will take care of me. You go on along."

The rain kept falling until the water was so high that Barney had to crawl up onto the roof of his house. He prayed again, "God, save me from this flood." A few minutes later some men in a motor-boat came by for Barney, but Barney refused to get in the boat. He had faith God would take care of him.

The water kept rising, and Barney felt it rushing over him as he clung to the chimney of his flooded house. "Lord," he prayed, "I have faith that you are going to save me from drowning." Just before the water got up to Barney's chest, he heard a whirling noise and then a voice over a loud speaker. The voice said, "Hey, mister, we'll throw a basket down to you. Hang on!" But Barney, steadfast in his faith, motioned for the helicopter to go away. You see, he knew that God would save him.

The rain continued to fall, the water continued to rise, and Barney, still praying, lost his hold on the chimney and drowned. When he got to heaven, he was met at heaven's gates by St. Peter. Barney had a disappointed look on his face. St. Peter said, "Barney, aren't heaven's gates as beautiful as you expected them to be?" Barney said, "St. Peter, it's not that. I just don't understand why I drowned. I prayed with faith that God would save me." St. Peter looked puzzled and said, "Well, Barney, God sent you two boats and a helicopter, but you refused the help."

Barney was like a lot of Christians are, he believed in prayer. He just never learned to watch and listen for God's answers.

Bible Verse:

The Bible verse today comes home **Colossians 4:2,** You say after me: **"Don't be weary in prayer; keep at it, watch for God's answers and remember to be thankful when they come."**

God answers prayers in many ways, but they usually aren't delivered on the wings of angels. More often than not, they are answered through the help of people. So, don't be surprised when God uses you to answer someone else's prayers.

Sermon Ending:

I brought each of you a little boat to help you remember the story about Barney so you will learn to watch and listen for answers to your prayers.

Devotional Ending:
Remember the story about Barney so you will learn to watch and listen for answers to your prayers.
Prayer:
Now, bow your head, close your eyes, and let's talk to God. You say after me: **"Dear God, Thank you for listening to me. Help me learn to listen for you. Amen."**

(You can find packets of plastic bathtub toy boats at toy stores, dollar stores, and in the Oriental Trade Catalog. *Helicopters tend to be sold in single units and are much more expensive.)*

#33
A Dirty Story
Based on Matthew 13: 1-23
(parable of the four soils)

THEME: Plant yourself in God's love and care, and you will grow into a strong, productive Christian.

I think it would be safe to say that everybody likes to hear a good story or read a good story or watch a good story. When we go to a movie theater, we watch a story being acted out, and most television shows are stories. People love stories.

When Jesus lived on earth, he was a very smart guy. He knew that the best way to get people to listen to him would be to tell them stories, and that is one of the ways Jesus taught people about how to act, how to live, and how to love. His stories were called parables. Say that word for me. PARABLES. A parable is a story that teaches a lesson. I am going to tell you one of Jesus' parables today. It's a dirty story. Let me rephrase that. It's a story about dirt. The story goes something like this:

There was a farmer who needed to plant seeds on his farm. Back then they didn't have tractors and big farm equipment to plant with, so this farmer just took handfuls of seeds and scattered them by hand. Some of the seeds the farmer scattered fell on a hard path, and the birds came and ate them. Some of the seeds fell where there were rocks in the dirt. Little plants grew, but they didn't live long because the dirt wasn't deep enough. There were too many rocks under the ground, and the roots couldn't grow, so they died. Other seeds fell into sticker bushes. When the little plants began to grow, the sticker bushes were so thick they choked them out. But some of the seeds fell on good dirt, and those plants took root and grew, producing lots and lots of grain — a whole lot more than he planted. THE END.

Now you may wonder why Jesus told that story. So did his disciples. They looked at Jesus and said, "What was that about?" So Jesus explained. He said that some people are like those seeds that fell on the hard path. They have a hard heart, and like those birds who ate the seeds, the devil eats away the goodness in their hearts. And some people are like the seeds that fell in the rocky dirt. They trust in God until they hit the rocky times, and then they don't like God anymore. They just don't have deep enough roots. Other people are like those seeds that fell in the sticker bushes. They grow with God, but eventually they let things like money and stuff become more important than God, and soon, just like the sticker bushes, it chokes God right out of their lives. But some people are like the seeds that fell in the good dirt. They grow and take root in God, and they lead others to God.

You are like a little plant. You are growing and spreading roots. If you decide to love God, trust God, and thank God, you will grow into a strong Christian who can make this world a better place by leading others to God.

Bible Verse:

The Bible verse today comes from **Matthew 13:8**. You say after me: **"Some seeds fell on good dirt, and produced a crop that was 100 times more than he planted."**

Sermon Ending:

I brought each of you some seeds to plant. Plant them in different kinds of places and see which ones grow and thrive and turn into plants. As you are planting your seeds, remember to keep yourself planted in God's love and care, and you will grow up to be a strong and productive Christian.

Devotional Ending:

Keep yourself planted in God's love and care, and you will grow up to be a strong and productive Christian.

Prayer:

Now, bow your head, close your eyes, and let's talk to God. You say after me: **"Dear God, Help me to grow into a strong and loving Christian. Help me lead others to you. Amen."**

(Use any kind of seeds you like, however, green beans can be bought at a feed store by the handfuls, which is cheaper than packages of seeds, and they are large enough for small children to handle. Also, they sprout quickly.)

#34

The Doer And The Talker
Based on Matthew 21:28-32, and Luke 3:8
(the parable of the two sons)

THEME: Repentance has two sides to it.

I want to tell you a story about a doer and talker. Jesus told this story, and it's about a man with two sons. This man, you see, had a farm, and he needed some work done on it. So, he went to his oldest boy and said, "Son, I need you to go out and do some work for me on the farm." But the boy said, "No, I just don't feel like it today. I have other things I want to do." So the farmer went out and found his younger boy and asked him to do the work for him, and that son said, "I'll be glad to, Dad."

Just a little while later, the oldest son started thinking about his Dad and all the work that needed to be done, and he changed his mind. He decided he shouldn't have talked to his Dad like he had, and he went out to the farm and did the work his Daddy had asked him to do. As the day passed, the youngest son who had told his Daddy he would work for him, never got around to it.

Which son ended up minding his Daddy? The oldest one — sure. That was the point Jesus was trying to make to the people he was telling this parable to: Saying you are going to do the right thing isn't the same as doing the right thing.

It's not good to say "No" to your Mom or Dad if they ask you to do something, but it is much worse to say you'll do it and know that you really aren't going to.

I'm going to teach you a new word today. It is a word that everyone needs to know and understand and practice. The word is REPENTANCE. Say it for me — REPENTANCE. Repentance simply means feeling sorry for something you have done wrong. Saying you are sorry and truly feeling sorry are not the same thing, and the deal is — God knows the difference every time.

You see, the oldest son in the story felt sorry for the way he had treated his dad, and he did something about it. Jesus wants you to be that way. When you make mistakes, or if you talk or act ugly, stop and think about it, ask for forgiveness, and then do the right thing.

Repentance has two sides to it. One side is to change what you are doing wrong, and the other side is to ask for forgiveness and mean it in your heart.

Bible Verse:

The Bible verse today comes from **Luke 3:8**. You say after me: **"Go and prove by the way you live that you really have repented."**

Sermon Ending:

Be doers — not just talkers. You may have heard the old saying: "There are two sides to every coin." Well, I'm going to give you a coin. It's to remind you that there are two sides to repentance. One side is to change what you are doing wrong, and the other side is to ask God to forgive you and mean it in your heart.

Devotional Ending:

Be doers — not just talkers. You may have heard the old saying: "There are two sides to every coin." The next time you find a penny, keep it to remind you that there are two sides to repentance just as there are two sides to that coin. One side is to change what you are doing wrong, and the other side is to ask God to forgive you and mean it in your heart.

Prayer:

Now, bow your head, close your eyes, and let's talk to God. You say after me: **"Dear God, Help me to say the right things and help me to do the right things. Amen."**

(You may want to use real coins, such as pennies, nickels or quarters, or you can order plastic coins from the Oriental Trading Catalog *which even has coins with a religious theme on either side.)*

#35

Be Prepared
Based on Matthew 25:1-13
(parable of the ten virgins)

THEME: We don't know what is in our future; be prepared with Jesus.

(The following is a personal story that you may use or you could certainly substitute your own story about a time when you were not prepared.) I want to tell you a story about a lady who went through something frightening because she wasn't prepared. She teaches prisoners inside a prison how to read. She goes to work at 4:30 in the morning, and it is still very dark that early. One morning she headed out for work during a bad storm. There was thunder and lightning and rain, and the wind was blowing very hard. She was glad to finally get inside her classroom and out of the storm. Her twenty-five students soon came in the room. Most of the prisoners had been in her class for awhile, and she knew them fairly well, but she also knew that they were in prison for doing some very naughty things — even scary things — like hurting people, and some had even killed people.

Goldfish and Silver Kisses

She started her lesson, the storm was blowing and going, it was still dark outside, and all of a sudden, the lights went out. It was so dark that she couldn't see anything. She knew that the prison had emergency generators, but that morning they did not come on. No lights!

The teacher found her way to her desk drawer and found her flashlight. *(Bring out a flashlight here.)* She was very relieved until she discovered the batteries were dead, and then she got scared! There she was, the only woman in the department, in a room full of criminals, in the dark, and she wasn't prepared. So like a scared little rabbit, she crawled under her desk and kept very quiet until a security officer came by with his flashlight.

Jesus told a story about some women who were not prepared. They didn't have flashlights back then. They carried lamps something like this that burned oil. *(You can find lamps like this in antique stores, over the internet, or you might ask your pastor where to find one. Mine is made from clay. If you can't find an oil lamp, bring a picture of one.)* The women in Jesus' parable were on their way to a wedding, but the wedding didn't start when they thought it was going to because the bridegroom was late. Some of the women had not prepared for that, and their lamps ran out of oil. While they were out buying more oil, the wedding took place without them. They missed out on the wedding and the wedding feast.

Jesus told that story to make this point. We don't know the future, and we don't know what is going to happen from one minute to the next. Jesus doesn't want you to run out of time before you make him Lord of your life. He doesn't want you to wait until you are married or wait until you have children or wait until you have a good job or wait until you retire to worship him. You see, your light could go out before you think it's going to, and if that were to happen, you wouldn't find yourself under a desk in a dark prison, and you wouldn't just miss out on a wedding party, you would miss out on heaven. That would be the most terrible and horrible thing that could ever happen to you.

Bible Verse:

The Bible verse today comes from **Matthew 25:13**. You say after me: **"Stay awake and be prepared, for you do not know the date or moment of my return."**

Sermon Ending:

I made each of you a little wedding cake to eat after lunch. Some of the women in Jesus' story missed out on their piece of wedding cake because their lamps went out, and they didn't get to the wedding on time. Don't be like those women. Be prepared. Be ready for Jesus.

Devotional Ending:

Be prepared. Be ready for Jesus.

Prayer:

Now, bow your head, close your eyes, and let's talk to God. You say after me: **"Dear God, Help me keep my light and my life burning bright for Jesus. Amen."**

(For the wedding cakes, I made cupcakes out of white cake mix. You can find canned snow-white frosting in the wedding cake/floral department of Walmart, or in stores that carry cake decorating items. They will also have miniature decorative wedding bands. I placed two on the top of each cupcake. Frost the cupcakes the night before so the frosting will harden enough so that you can put each cupcake in a zip-lock bag.)

#36
A Talent Of Talent
Based on Matthew 25:14-30
(the parable of the loaned money)

THEME: Be the best YOU that you can be.

This lesson in based on another one of the parables Jesus told. It is about a man who gave some talents to his servants to invest. God has given each of you something to invest for him. It is something you were given even before you were born. Some of you might know what it is already, and some of you may not know what it is for a long time. It too is called a talent.

In the Bible story, a talent is a unit of money, but the kind of talent God gave you is the kind that means the ability to do something really well. It is something that will come easy for you, naturally. If you invest your talent, in other words, if you spend your talent on Godly things, it will get better and better and better.

All my life I have heard people say, "You can do anything or be anything you want if you just put your mind to it and work at it hard enough." I am here to tell you — that is just not true.

(You may need to use different examples from the following.) I could have spent my life, day in and day out, training to become a professional football player, and I wouldn't have made it. I could practice singing every day of the world, and I still wouldn't be able to sing like Ms. Barbara, our music director, and that might be the same for you. You may never be able to sing well or play football, but there is something you will be able to do well, and God will show it to you if you are open to him. When you discover your talent, God wants you to work hard to improve it and invest it; spend it on Godly things.

You might have a talent for saving money. (I wish I did.) A person like that could volunteer to be on the church finance committee. You might someday discover that you have a real talent for cooking. A person like that could cook food for people who are sick or don't have enough to eat. Your talent might be to melt a person's heart with a smile, and just by coming to church you could give someone the strength to keep going just when they needed it most.

Bible Verse:

The Bible verse today comes from **Matthew 25:29**. You say after me: **"For the man who uses well what he is given shall be given more, and he shall have abundance."**

God doesn't expect you to be and act like somebody you are not. He just wants you to be the best YOU that you can be. He loves you, and he made you who you are for a reason. He molded you with a special talent, a gift. Take that talent and work to make it better, and then invest it in Godly things.

Sermon Ending:

I brought each of you some craft dough to play with. As you mold it into different things, let it remind you that God molded each of you with your very own special talent. Use it wisely.

Devotional Ending:

As our Bible verse says — for those who use their talent well,

God will give them more of it.

Prayer:

Now, bow your head, close your eyes, and let's talk to God. You say after me: **"Dear God, Help me to mold my talent and use it for Godly things. Amen."**

(Art/play/craft dough can be bought several cans to a packet. Walmart and most toy, craft, or dollar stores will have it.)

#37
The Crown Of Life
Based on Mark 10:32-34

THEME: Your future is the crown of life if you trust and believe in Jesus.

Have you ever wished you could tell the future? You know, be able to know what was going to happen before it happens? *(The following is a personal story which you can use, or you could substitute one of your own.)* When I was little, I thought that would be so neat because I would know about all the good things coming my way. For example, I would be able to tell what was in all my Christmas packages before I even opened them. Or like the time I got lost in the woods behind our house, I would have known that my dog, Beano, would help me find my way home, and I wouldn't have been so afraid. Or, I would have known who I was going to marry even before I ever met the guy, and I wouldn't have had to go through the trouble of dating other boys until the right guy showed up.

Just think of all the worry and trouble it would save you if you could tell the future — or would it?

If you knew what was in all your Christmas packages even before you opened them, wouldn't that spoil the anticipation and the fun and excitement of opening them to see what was inside? And you know what — if I had been able to know that my dog, Beano, was going to get me out of the woods, I would also have known that he would get hit by a car and killed the very next day.

And if I had known who I was going to marry even before I met him, perhaps I wouldn't have dated other guys, and I wouldn't realize just how special the man I married is, because I wouldn't have anything to compare him to. Seeing into the future has two sides, doesn't it?

If you could see into the future, it would spoil your surprises, it would probably cause you deep sadness and dread, and you wouldn't be able to appreciate and enjoy the good in your life for trying to prevent the bad. Knowing the future would be a burden.

I know someone who could see into the future. This person even knew when he was going to die, and he knew how it would happen, and he knew how mean people were going to be to him, and he knew how much he would hurt as he was dying. But instead of running from it and hiding, he faced his death with courage and with dignity and even with love for those who were going to kill him. His name was Jesus. His name is Jesus.

Bible Verse:

The Bible verse today comes from **Mark 10:33**. You say after me: **"They will mock me and spit on me and whip me and kill me."**

Do you want to hear the rest of that verse? Jesus says, "After three days I will come back to life again." That is why you and I have a future. Because Jesus died for us, we have been forgiven for what we do wrong, and because he lives again, we will live again in heaven after we die. So, in a way, you can see into the future, because if you believe in and love Jesus, you can be sure that you will have a home with him after you die on this earth.

In the first chapter of James, verse 12, it says, "Happy is the man who doesn't give in and do wrong when tempted, for afterwards he will get his reward — the crown of life that God has promised those who love him." That is the only future we need to see into.

Sermon Ending:

I brought each of you a crown today to remind you that your future is the crown of life if you trust and believe in Jesus.

Devotional Ending:

Trust and believe in Jesus. Let him be your crowning glory.

Prayer:

Now, bow your head, close your eyes, and let's talk to God. You say after me: **"Dear God, Thank you for the crown of life in my future. Thank you for Jesus. Amen."**

(Little paper crowns are easy to find at dollar stores, toy stores, or in the Oriental Trading Catalog.*)*

#38
God's Amazing Guidance
Based on Psalms 25:4

THEME: In life there will be obstacles.

Have you ever lost something? I have too. The other day I thought I had lost my reading glasses. I looked on my desk in the study, but they weren't there. I searched all the desk drawers, but I couldn't find them. I thought maybe I had left them in the den, so I went there, looked all over the room — high and low — but no glasses. I then went to the kitchen and looked on the counters. I went into the dining room and looked on the table, then to the utility room, but no glasses.

I stopped and tried to remember where I had last used them. I went into the music room and looked on top of the piano, then down the hall to my bedroom and looked beside my bed. I looked in my dressing room and on my dresser. Still, no glasses!

I searched my entire house. I had gone on a journey of sorts. I went from one room to the next — in some doors and out other doors. I even went to some places I had already been, thinking I had overlooked my glasses. Do you know where I finally found them? I found them when I saw my reflection in a mirror. They were right in front of my face. Actually, they were on my face.

Life is like that sometimes. We go from one place to the next in search of what we think we need when what we really need is right in front of us. It's something we've had all along but didn't realize it. When we go off on any journey, we need to remember what is important, and that is God's love and guidance.

Bible Verse:

The Bible verse today comes from **Psalms 25:4**. You say after me: "**Show me the path where I should go, O Lord; point out the right road for me to walk.**"

Sermon Ending:

I brought each of you a maze today. Let me show you how it works. You try to get the little ball from the starting line to the finish line. You will run into obstacles along the way. It's to remind you that in life there will be obstacles. Sometimes you will lose things and sometimes you might get lost yourself. Just remember to ask God for guidance. For you see, God is "a-**MAZ**-ing."

Devotional Ending:

You have probably seen a maze before. Sometimes they come in coloring or puzzle books. You enter the maze and try to find the pathway out, but you run into obstacles along the way. Your life will be a maze of sorts, and you will run into obstacles. Sometimes you will lose things, and sometimes you might get lost yourself. Just remember to ask God for guidance. For you see, God is "a-**MAZ**-ing!"

Prayer:

Now, bow your head, close your eyes, and let's talk to God. You say after me: "**Dear God, Guide us on every path we take. Amen.**"

(You can buy packets of those little mazes similar to pin ball machines without the pull knob at most toy stores in the party favors section or through the Oriental Trading Catalog.*)*

#39
Of Faith And Frogs
Based on Exodus, chapters 7-11, and Psalms 11:4
(plagues strike Egypt)

THEME: Don't be stubborn when it comes to God.

FAITH. Do you know what that means? Faith is when you believe in something even if you have never seen it. Have you ever seen God? Have you ever even seen a real picture of God? Well, if you and I have never seen God, how do we know he really exists?

The Bible tells us about a man, Pharaoh, in Egypt who didn't believe God existed, because he had never seen him. Pharaoh used the people of Israel as slaves in Egypt, and God wanted Pharaoh to let those people go.

God used a man named Moses and his brother Aaron to help him. I want you to listen to all the terrible things that had to happen before Pharaoh finally believed that God really existed and was the big guy in charge. Before I tell you what all happened, understand that before each terrible disaster, Moses warned Pharaoh what God was about to do if he didn't let his people go.

- First, God turned Aaron's rod into a snake. Pharaoh was not impressed.
- Then God turned all the water in Egypt into blood.
- He sent millions of frogs into Egypt, and they covered up everything.
- Then he turned the dust into lice, and they infested the people and all the animals. Still, Pharaoh was a non-believer.
- Swarms of flies came next, filling their homes and covering the ground.
- God caused the livestock that belonged to the Egyptians to die, but still Pharaoh would not let the slaves go free.
- Boils, painful and nasty sores, broke out on the Egyptians, covering their bodies.
- A hailstorm came, killing people, killing all the vegetation, their crops, leaving Egypt in ruins.
- Next God sent hordes of locusts to eat up everything the hailstorm had left.
- God caused Egypt to be in total darkness for three days and nights. It was so dark, the people who were left could not see to move.
- Then finally, when God caused the firstborn son of every Egyptian to die, Pharaoh listened to God, and let the people of Israel, the Hebrews, go free. It took all that to make him believe.

After hearing that story, do you think God wants us to believe in him, even if we have never seen him? I do.

Pharaoh was very stubborn. God used Moses and Aaron to try to make him listen, but he had never seen God and just didn't want to believe.

God uses people everyday to teach others about him. God may even use you to teach others about him.

Bible Verse:

The Bible verse comes from **Psalms 11:4**. You say after me:

"The Lord is still in his holy temple; he still rules from heaven."

Sermon Ending:

We have not seen God, but we must have faith that God is watching over us. God sees us. Remember from the story that one of the things God cursed Egypt with was millions of frogs? I brought each of you a frog to remind you not to be stubborn like that old Pharaoh.

Devotional Ending:

We have not seen God, but God sees us, and he is watching over us. Remember the story of the plagues God struck Egypt with, and strive to not be stubborn like that old Pharaoh.

Prayer:

Now, bow your head, close your eyes, and let's talk to God. You say after me: **"Dear God, Help me to be ever faithful to you. Amen."**

(You can buy plastic/rubber frogs at toy or dollar stores and in the Oriental Trading Catalog.*)*

#40
Storing Memories
Based on Deuteronomy 6:5, Matthew 22:37, Mark 12:30, Luke 10:27

THEME: Fill your memory store with Godly things.

When I need something at home, like milk and cereal, or meat and bread, I go to a grocery store to find and buy those items. If I need new tires for my car, I go to a tire store. If I need a new dress, I go to a clothing store. A store is a place where items are stored so people can go and find what they need or want.

Did you know that each of you have your very own store? Your store is right between your ears. It's your brain. Your brain is where you store memories, things that you want to remember. God wants you to remember him, and he wants you to remember Bible stories and Bible verses. But most or all, he wants you to remember that he loves you. God wants you to put him in your store so that you can go get him any time you want him or need him. God also wants you to tell others about his love for you and about your love for him which brings us to our Bible verse today.

Bible Verse:

The Bible verse is found in four different places in the Bible: **Deuteronomy 6:5, Matthew 22:37, Mark 12:30, and Luke 10:27,** so it must be very important. You say after me: **"Love the Lord thy God with all your heart, with all your soul, and with all your mind."**

When I go to the grocery store, I usually take a list to help me remember the things I need. It is a reminder. Reminders are very helpful, (and that is why I give you little tokens or treats after each lesson, to help you remember things we have talked about. They are to help you store memories.) (*Omit the part in parentheses if you use the devotional endings.*)

Put God in your memory store. Remember to love God with all your heart, soul, and mind. If you talk about God, think about God, and worship God, your memory store will fill up with Godly things, and God will bless you for that.

Sermon Ending:

I brought each of you a little scroll today. Inside it is printed the Bible verse for today. Memorize it. Put it in your memory store, and think about it often. It will bring you closer to God.

Devotional Ending:

Try to memorize a Bible verse every week. Put it in your memory store, and think about it often. It will bring you closer to God.

Prayer:

Now, bow your head, close your eyes, and let's talk to God. You say after me: **"Dear God, Live in my memory, guide my future, rule my heart. Amen."**

(*I used the scroll idea from the "Bible Fun for Everyone" book. See my introduction for where to find this craft book. This was a great project.*)

#41
Heart Of Gold
Based on Isaiah 1:1-20 and Matthew 15: 8-9

THEME: God doesn't like fakes.

    As people get older, they generally get smarter about things. They learn about things just by living. They learn by going to school and then by working. They learn from other people, and they learn by doing. They learn by making mistakes, and they learn by trying over and again to get things right. That is why old people act smarter and are smarter than young people. They have had more practice at "life-stuff."

    But there is something children, people your age, are smarter about than old people. Little children tend to know whether or not someone truly likes them. You guys have some sort of radar detector that lets you know if someone is genuinely good or if they are just pretending to be.

    When someone is pretending to like you, but they really don't, we say they are a fake. There are fake things as well as fake people. Take sugar for instance. If you were to give me a diet Coke and tell me it was a regular Coke, trust me, I would know the difference. It does not taste like the real thing. There are fake diamonds, fake money, fake fingernails, fake hair, fake fur, fake gold, and the list could go on and on. Something fake is just not the same as or as valuable as the real thing.

All fake things aren't necessarily bad. A lot of women wear fake fingernails, and I just love them, but there are fake things that are bad. *(If you are a man presenting this lesson, you will probably want to use a different example.)* One in particular is so bad that the Bible says it makes God sick, and that is fake love in someone's heart.

God is even better at knowing who loves him than little children are. The Bible tells us that God does not like it when people pretend to love him, but in their heart they really don't. God doesn't like it when people are fakes.

Bible Verse:

The Bible verse today comes from **Matthew 15:8-9**. You say after me: **"These people say they honor me, but their hearts are far away. Their worship is worthless."**

In the first chapter of Isaiah, it tells us to learn to do good, to be fair, and to help others. It tells us to care about God and to appreciate all he does for us. It says that when we mess up, to truly be sorry for it; don't just pretend to be. Don't be a fake.

Sermon Ending:

I brought each of you something that looks like gold and has been mistaken for real gold so often that it came to be known as fool's gold. Real gold is pure and precious and beautiful and valuable, but this is fake. It is pretty to look at, but it's not worth very much. It's not the real thing. Let it remind you to be worth something to God. Don't be fake. Show God true and real love from your heart.

Devotional Ending:

Have you ever heard of fool's gold. It sort of resembles gold, but it doesn't have the same qualities. Real gold is pure and precious and beautiful and valuable while fool's gold is fake. It is pretty to look at, but it is not worth very much; it is not the real thing. Be like real gold to God. Be worth something; don't be fake.

Prayer:

Now, bow your head, close your eyes, and let's talk to God. You say after me: **"Dear God, Give me a heart of gold. Make me precious in your eyes. Amen."**

(I found little bags of fool's gold at Michael's, the craft and hobby store. Don't forget the internet as a good source to find things.)

#42
Wisdom And Common Sense
Based on Proverbs 4:7

THEME: Wisdom and common sense will keep you on the right path.

(Presenter needs to have a live goldfish in a jar preferably with a lid.) I brought a guest with me today. His name is Mr. Foolish Fish. Look into his jar. Where do you think he's going? If he swims any faster, do you think he'll get there any quicker?

I've known some people like Mr. Foolish Fish. They just sort of move in circles going nowhere. They have no plans; they have no hope. They end up where they started from and make no difference on the trip — just like this sad little foolish fish.

God doesn't want us to have lives like this fish. He wants us to lead happy and full lives. He wants us to go places, see and do new and exciting things, and he wants us to make a difference in this world.

God tells us in the Bible that there are two goals we must work towards on our life's journey or our life's trip. The first is *wisdom*. Wisdom means knowing what is right and then doing what is right. The second goal is *common sense*; think before you do. The Bible tells us that wisdom and common sense will fill you with energy and bring you honor and respect. It says it will keep you from stumbling off the right path.

Bible Verse:

The Bible verse today comes from **Proverbs 4:7.** You say after me: "**Getting wisdom is the most important thing you can do. Develop common sense and good judgement.**"

The Bible goes on to tell us how to learn wisdom and common sense. It says to listen to your parents, stay away from wicked people, choose friends that are good and helpful to others, and to pray for wisdom and common sense.

Sermon Ending:

Your parents are praying this very minute that I had the common sense not to bring each of you a goldfish! I thought about it and decided to bring you some *Goldfish crackers* instead. Let them remind you to not be like Mr. Foolish Fish — just going around in circles. Be wise, and use common sense, and that will take you places.

Devotional Ending:

Don't be like Mr. Foolish Fish, just spending your life going around in circles. Be wise, and use common sense. That will take you places!

Prayer:

Now, bow you head, close your eyes, and let's talk to God. You say after me: "**Dear God, Teach me wisdom and common sense. Help me to recognize those traits in others. Amen.**"

(Goldfish crackers come in individual packets and cartons.)

#43
Giving God
Based on Acts 4:31-35

THEME: Sharing feels good!

I want to talk to you about sharing and giving today. Have you ever been told to share? Let me tell you why it is so important to share. When you share with people, you are sharing with God. God created people, and he loves them. God lives in them through Jesus and the Holy Spirit if they allow him to.

When you share what you have, not only are you sharing with God, you are actually sharing God. When you give to someone, you are giving God. When you help someone, you are helping God. When you love someone, you are loving God.

You can't truly love God without giving God. You can't love God if you don't have the ability to love others. You can't understand God's grace if you can't forgive others, and you can't fully appreciate the blessings God has given you until you learn to share your blessings with others.

Bible Verse:

The Bible verse today comes from **Acts 4:32**. You say after me: **"The group of believers was one in mind and heart. They all shared with one another everything they had."**

Did you know that sharing makes you feel good if you do it with a loving heart? Have you ever given someone a present and then could hardly wait to see if they like it? Well, when the feeling you get is better when you give than it is when you receive, that means God is working inside you.

Prayer:

Let's talk to God, and then I have an assignment for you. Bow your head and close your eyes. You say after me: **"Dear God, Give me the desire to share with others. Bless others through me. Amen."**

Sermon Ending:

I am going to give you the opportunity to see how good it feels to share and give today. I have a chocolate rose for each of you. I want you to find someone in this church that you don't know to give your rose to, and it must be done before this next hymn is over.

Devotional Ending:

Find an opportunity to see how good it feels to share and give this week. Give a flower to someone you don't know, or draw a picture, and take it to an elderly person in a nursing home. Perhaps you could take one of your toys and donate it to a shelter or an orphanage.

Now, go forth and share God by giving to someone, and let it make you feel good!

(I bought the chocolate roses after Valentine's Day for 50% off. Real or artificial flowers or even wrapped home-made cookies would do just as well, but it needs to be something the children would like to have for themselves.)

(If this is not being done in a church, you might ask the child or children to give their gift to someone in a nursing home or seniors' center.)

#44
Making Memories With God
Based on Joshua 4

THEME: Who is Lord of your life?

I want to talk to you about making memories today. Your memory is simply your store of what you remember. Sometimes memories are kept by taking pictures of an event, like at a birthday party or on family vacations. Another way to remember a specific place or event is by bringing back a souvenir. *(Presenter will want to bring a personal souvenir to show the children in place of the one I mention here.)* When I was nine years old, my parents took me to Arizona. They bought me this turquoise ring as a souvenir. This ring brings back memories of that vacation for me.

A good way to remember a person is by building a memorial to them. There are lots of memorials in cemeteries where family members have placed tombstones at the site where a loved one is buried. They can go to that place and recall memories of a person they knew and loved.

In the Bible there is a story about a memorial. It was a memorial that God instructed a man named Joshua to have built. Joshua was the man who helped Moses bring the Israelites out of the slavery of Egypt and all the way to Canaan, the land God had promised them. That was a very long and difficult journey where God performed many miracles for his people. When they finally reached the Promised Land, there was only one more obstacle in their way. It was the Jordan River, and it was flooded. God performed yet another miracle for his people by parting the water so the Israelites could cross over on dry land. God wanted the people to have a memory of this, so he told Joshua to have twelve men each get a stone from the Jordan River and build a memorial to him with those stones.

God wanted the memorial to remind the people of how he dried up the river right before their eyes and kept it dry until they were all across. God wanted a memorial to remind Israel that he was their Lord and is the Lord over all the earth.

Bible Verse:

The Bible verse today comes from **Joshua 4:21-22**. You say after me: **"Your children will ask, 'What do these stones mean?' Then you can tell them, 'This is where the Israelites crossed the Jordan on dry ground.'"**

We do all sorts of things in life to help us remember the fun we have had, the places we have been, or the people we have loved, but how many of us make memories for God?

Sermon Ending:

I brought each of you a memorial today. It is a cross with the words "God is Love" printed on it. Put it in a special place where you will see it everyday. Let it remind you of who is Lord of your life, and begin making memories with God.

Devotional Ending:

Find a stone or some other object that you can put in a place that is special to you. Let it remind you of who is Lord of your life. Add stones or other objects to your memorial as you make memories with God.

Prayer:

Now, bow your head, close your eyes, and let's talk to God. You say after me: **"Dear God, As you help me cross through each day, fill my heart with memories of your love and grace. Amen."**

(From the Oriental Trading Catalog, *I ordered the glow-in-the-dark crosses on a black pedestal. You may prefer to give stones, depending on the ages and personalities of the children you are teaching.)*

#45
Oh, My God
Based on Matthew 11:25-28 and Psalms 46:10

THEME: Belief in God must be more than just an idea.

    I read a story once that was told by an evangelist, a preacher, by the name of Reverend George Whitehead. Reverend Whitehead asked this man he met what he believed, and the man said, "I believe what my church believes." Reverend Whitehead asked, "And what is it that your church believes?" The man thought and said, "My church believes what I believe." Reverend Whitehead asked, "Well, what is it that you both believe?" The man looked at him seriously and said, "We both believe the same thing."

    If someone were to ask you what you believe, I hope you can say, I believe in God, and I believe that God made the heavens and the earth and all that is in them. I hope you can say, I believe that God made me, that God knows everything about me, and that God loves me.

    Believing and trusting in God is the most important thing you can do, and God loves the way little children do that. You see, children, like you, take God as he is and don't feel the need to understand all the mysteries and questions of the universe in order to make a decision about their belief in God, as some grown-ups come to do. You simply believe that God is God and that is all you need to know.

Bible Verse:

The Bible verse today comes from **Psalms 46:10**. You say after me: **"Be still and know that I am God."**

That is (one of) my favorite verse in the whole Bible because whenever I have a problem or get angry or sick or sad, I can put that problem up next to God, and it doesn't look quite so big. I get still and think about how powerful my God is, and I believe that God will go with me through any problem that comes my way.

Belief in God can't be just an idea. True belief in God means that you have a relationship with him. The more you talk to God and trust in God, the more powerful God will become in your life. You will understand that God truly lives and rules over all the universe.

Sermon Ending:

I brought each of you a little puzzle today to remind you that your life will be puzzling at times. Problems will arise that will make you wonder what to do and which way to turn. Just remember to always turn to God. At those times, just stop what you're doing, get still, and know that he really is GOD. You will find your problems won't look so big after that.

Devotional Ending:

Your life will be puzzling at times. Problems will arise that will make you wonder what to do and which way to turn. Just remember to always turn to God. At those times, just stop what you're doing, get still, and know that he really is GOD. You will find your problems won't look so big after that.

Prayer:

Now, bow your head, close your eyes, and let's talk to God. You say after me: "**Dear God, I believe in your power, in your promises, and in your love. I believe in you. Amen.**"

(My puzzles came from the Oriental Trading Catalog *and were the plastic kind with one square missing The puzzle requires that you slide the pieces around to form the picture. I was fortunate enough to be given a large box full of toys and tokens that I have described in this book and used, including the ones above, by a friend who found out about my sermons and wanted to help. Thanks Sylvia!)*

#46
Oh, My Goodness
Based on Titus 1:15 and Psalms 119:9

THEME: Look for the good in others instead of the bad.

(Presenter needs to be wearing sunglasses.) What am I wearing on my face? Sunglasses, that's right. Why do people wear sunglasses? They wear them to filter out some of the glare and brightness from the sun so they can see things more clearly.

Our souls are a bit like sunglasses. Our souls are filters through which we see goodness and evil. Let me explain what your soul is. Your soul is your feelings. It's who you are even if you didn't have a body. Your soul is the part of you that will go to heaven someday to be with God.

God wants our souls, our feelings, to be full of good and pure thoughts. Listen to what the Bible tells us in the book of Titus 1:15. "A person who is pure of heart sees goodness and purity in everything; but a person whose own heart is evil and untrusting finds evil in everything, for his dirty mind and rebellious heart color all he sees and hears."

When you act good, your soul has good feelings, and the

more often you act good, the fuller your soul gets with purity and goodness. A pure and good soul allows you to filter through the bad and see goodness in others. Fill your soul with good and there will be little room for bad.

Bible Verse:

The Bible verse today comes from **Psalms 119:9.** You say after me: "**How can a young person stay pure? By reading the Bible and following its rules.**"

Sermon Ending:

I brought each of you some sunglasses today. When you wear them, I want you to practice looking for the goodness in others instead of the bad. The more goodness you see, the fuller your soul gets with goodness.

Devotional Ending:

Practice looking for goodness in others instead of the bad. The more goodness you see, the fuller your soul gets with goodness.

Prayer:

Now, bow your head, close your eyes, and let's talk to God. You say after me: "**Dear God, Help me fill my mind with pure thoughts and my soul with goodness. Amen.**"

(You can find children's plastic sunglasses in packages in dollar stores or toy stores or the Oriental Trading Catalog.*)*

#47

For Big Mistakes
Based on Luke 6:37

THEME: God allows us to make mistakes so we can see our blessings.

Have you ever made a really big mistake? I have. I made one just the other day, and it was because I had let something steal my joy that should have given me joy to begin with. Let me start from the beginning. I had just gotten a check for over $500.00 for some consulting work I had done one Saturday morning in Dallas. I had thought of a hundred things I wanted to buy with that money, but the day after I received the check, it rained really hard on my way home from work. I could hardly keep my Jeep on the road; I knew I needed new tires.

The next day I went to the tire store and discovered that four new tires would cost over $500.00. There went my extra money that I had wanted to use for fun stuff — you know — the kind of stuff you just want, but don't need. I was pouting about it while on the way to Walmart to buy some other things I needed but didn't really want.

After shopping, I rolled the cart out to my Jeep. While still pouting, I began putting my groceries in the back of my Jeep, leaving my wallet in the shopping cart. BIG MISTAKE! I turned around and it was gone. $35.00, my checkbook, a number of credit cards, my driver's license, social security card, and a gold Cross pen, given to me with my name on it — all gone. It took me all afternoon to cancel my credit cards and take care of losing my social security card with four different government agencies.

Bible Verse:

The Bible verse today comes from **Romans 8:28**. You say after me: **"We know that God causes everything to work together for the good of those who love God."**

You see, instead of being grateful to God that I'd had the opportunity to make five hundred extra dollars, giving me almost exactly what I needed for new tires, I was pouting because that is what I had to spend the money on. God had blessed me, and I was too blind to see it or appreciate it. God knew I needed new tires before I did, and he had provided a way for me to pay for them. My really big mistake wasn't that I turned my back on my wallet where it could be stolen. My mistake was failing to see how carefully and lovingly God takes care of me. New tires could have very well saved my life, and losing a purse taught me an important lesson about my life. I need to be grateful for God's blessings and understand that all things work together for good to them that love God.

Sermon Ending:

I brought each of you an eraser today for REALLY BIG MISTAKES. Let it remind you that God sometimes lets us make mistakes in order that we can erase the selfishness that clouds our blessings from God.

Devotional Ending:

God sometimes lets us make really big mistakes so that we can erase the selfishness that clouds our blessings from God.

Prayer:

Now, bow your head, close your eyes, and let's talk to God. You say after me: **"Dear God, When I make big mistakes, erase what has caused them so that I may see your blessings more clearly. Amen."**

(The Oriental Trading Catalog *has large 6 by 2 inch erasers with the words, FOR BIG MISTAKES printed on them. They are sold by the dozen.)*

#48
Strength Of Fortune
Based on Nehemiah 8:10

THEME: God's word and God's joy can be your strength.

Listen carefully to this question. How much of what you do today will be to please God? How many of your actions will be done with the purpose of making God proud of you? Can you imagine what our town would be like if even for one day every person living here got up out of bed with that question in mind and then spent that day pleasing God? I can promise you, without a doubt, if that were to happen for only one day, enough goodness would arise in our community that it would make the national news, even the world news.

Did you know that when you try consciously to please God, you are the one who gets filled with joy? The more of it you give, the more of it you get. That is quite a deal when you think about it.

Bible Verse:

The Bible verse today comes from **Nehemiah 8:10**. You say after me: **"The joy of the Lord is your strength."**

Let's think about that verse for a minute. "The joy of the Lord is your strength." I think that means that when we try to please God — try to make God happy with us — in return, God strengthens us. For every kind and good thing we do, we gain strength from God. I'm not talking about big muscle strength, I'm talking about strength of spirit, strength of character, strength of heart and soul. Those are kinds of strengths you will need the most as you grow up. Those strengths will carry you through any situation, no matter how tough because those are the strengths that keep you in touch with God.

It doesn't take a whole town to bring about goodness or change or joy. If only one of you sitting here with me got up tomorrow with the purpose of trying to please God all day, you have no idea what a difference that could make — differences you may never become aware of, but differences that God will be aware of. Why don't you try it?

Sermon Ending:

I brought each of you a fortune cookie today. A fortune cookie usually contains a strip of paper that supposedly gives you an idea of what is in your future. These fortune cookies contain a strip of paper with a Bible verse that will definitely give you an idea of what is in your future. You see, God's word, God's joy is your strength. Make that your future.

Devotional Ending:

Learn verses from the Bible. God's word and God's joy is your strength. Make that your future.

Prayer:

Now, bow your head, close your eyes, and let's talk to God. You say after me: **"Dear God, Give me the desire and the will to please you. Strengthen me with your joy. Amen."**

(The fortune cookies containing the Bible verses came from the Oriental Trading Catalog.)

#49
The Right Kind
Based on Matthew 5:9

THEME: Sometimes it is better to be kind than right.

I don't like to be wrong, do you? Most people don't. We don't like for anyone to tell us we are wrong. It makes us mad, and it hurts our feelings. It causes people to fuss and fight because people like to be right, and they want to believe that their opinions are right. People disagreeing about what is right and what is wrong, and who is right and who is wrong, has caused the world's biggest problems. The argument between who is right and who is wrong causes love to turn into hate, marriage to turn into divorce, beauty to turn into ugliness, and peace to turn into war.

Bible Verse:

The Bible verse today comes from **Matthew 5:9.** You say after me: **"Blessed are the peacemakers, for they shall be called the children of God."**

God wants us to do the right thing and live the right way. He doesn't want us to give in to wrong, but he wants us to do what is right in a peaceful way. He wants us to live right instead of demanding that others believe we are right.

Telling someone they are wrong isn't necessarily your responsibility. You have to realize that your feelings about a situation are not always a measure of its rightness or wrongness. Two people can look at one thing and see something totally different.

Your life, if you try to live for God, can show others what is right, and your life may be the only Christianity some people get a dose of.

There are times when it is better to be kind than right about something. Kindness goes a long way toward changing someone's attitude. God will use you in ways you won't even be aware of. He will use you to bring about love, joy, and peace for others — a peacemaker — but first there must be kindness.

Sermon Ending:

I brought each of you a ruler today that has "The Golden Rule" printed on it because a ruler is a tool we use to measure with. Let it be a reminder that your feelings aren't always a measure of someone else's rightness or wrongness. Live for God. Measure what is right by him, and let him judge the feelings of others.

Devotional Ending:

Remember that your feelings aren't always a measure of someone else's rightness or wrongness. Live for God. Measure what is right by him, and let him judge the feelings of others.

Prayer:

Now, bow your head, close your eyes, and let's talk to God. You say after me: **"Dear God, Help me live by the golden rule and treat others the way I want to be treated with kindness. Amen."**

(The rulers with The Golden Rule printed on them are available in the Oriental Trading Catalog.*)*

#50
Fall for Goodness' Sake
Based on I Peter 3:16

THEME: Your reputation isn't so much what you stand for — it's what you fall for.

Have any of you ever played "Follow the Leader" or "Simon Says?" Both are fun games that I used to play when I was a child, where you either follow where the leader goes, or do what Simon says to do. Games are great, but it is important to understand the difference between a game and real life.

In real life situations, it is never good to follow someone without knowing where they are headed. It is not good to follow someone just because your friends follow. When you do what your friends are doing, and you know that what they are doing is wrong, it can ruin your reputation. REPUTATION. Say that for me — REPUTATION. Your reputation is what people think about your character — whether you are a good person or a bad person. Your reputation is what allows people to trust you or be leery of you.

No matter how good you are, there will be those who call

you names and say ugly things about you. People even did that to Jesus. However, the trick is to live and behave so that others will not believe it.

Bible Verse:

The Bible verse today comes from **I Peter 3:16**. You say after me: **"Do what is right; then if men speak against you, calling you evil names, they will become ashamed of themselves for falsely accusing you when you have only done what is good."**

You can go to church, be helpful to others, make good grades, and stand up for what is right, but if you let people talk you into doing the wrong thing by saying, "just once won't hurt anything," you could really hurt your reputation. I heard it once said that your reputation isn't so much what you stand for — it's what you fall for.

Jesus was talked about, ridiculed, and even killed for what he stood for, and there are still people today who choose not to invite him into their hearts. However, you would have to look far and wide to find somebody who would not say he was a good person. There are those who may not believe his miracles or in his purpose for being on earth, but few will deny his goodness. You see, Jesus didn't fall for things that would bring disgrace to his character or to God's. He came face to face with the devil himself and did not fall for the devil's temptations.

Sermon Ending:

I brought each of you a little flashlight that has "Jesus is the light and the way," printed on it. If you are going to follow someone, follow Jesus. If you are going to lead someone, lead them to Jesus. Build your reputation around his light, and live that others may see that light in you.

Devotional Ending:

If you are going to follow someone, follow Jesus. If you are going to lead someone, lead them to Jesus. Build your reputation around his light, and live that others may see that light in you.

Prayer:

Now, bow your head, close your eyes, and let's talk to God. You say after me: **"Dear God, help me live so that others will see goodness in me. Amen."**

(I found the flashlights in the Oriental Trading Catalog *in the religious section.)*

#51
A Patient Of Patience
Based on Psalms 46:10

THEME: Learn to be patient. God is in control.

I want to talk to you about a particular word today, and that word is PATIENCE. Say it for me: PATIENCE. Patience is the ability to wait for something calmly. That is a very hard thing for many of us to do. It is hard for me to wait for things. Like, if I go on a diet on Monday, I want those extra pounds gone by Tuesday. If something I use quits working, I want it repaired immediately, or I want a new one. I have found myself becoming frustrated because the screen on my computer doesn't change in a split second when I am using the internet, and before the internet and before home computers, I had to spend hours in a library looking up the same information. I need more patience!

I prayed about it. I prayed, "Dear God, help me to be more patient, **and do it right this very minute!**" I realized something after I prayed that prayer. God has the utmost patience. Think about it. God has all of us down here on earth to deal with, yet

God is never out of control. He is never late, he is never early; he is always right on time. Even though we want God to fix things in our lives that are broken, and we want him to fix them right now, God knows the right time, and he waits for the right time. You see, God always answers our prayers; they just aren't always the answers we want to hear when we want to hear them.

God is in control. He knows things about the future that we don't. He knows what is best for us when often we don't. He makes us wait for things so we can grow more patient and more understanding and more obedient. Thank goodness, God is patient with us.

Bible Verse:

The Bible verse today comes from **Psalms 46:10**. You say after me: **"Be still and know that I am God."**

Doesn't that verse make you feel safe? The next time you have trouble waiting for something, think about that verse. Just get still for a minute and think about God. Have faith that no matter what happens or doesn't happen, God is always in control.

Sermon Ending:

I brought each of you a spinning top today. Our lives are sometimes like this toy. We want things faster and faster, we want God to fix things faster, and before you know it, we are spinning out of control. When that happens, be still and know that God really is God.

Devotional Ending:

Sometimes our lives are like a spinning toy top. We want things faster and faster, we want God to fix things faster, and before you know it, we are spinning out of control. When that happens, be still and know that God really is God.

Prayer:

Now, bow your head, close your eyes, and let's talk to God. You say after me: **"Dear God, Bless me with a patient spirit and an understanding heart. Amen."**

Goldfish and Silver Kisses

(Little plastic spinning tops can be purchased by the gross in the Oriental Trading Catalog, but dollar stores and toy stores have them in smaller quantities.)

#52
A New Pair Of Eyes
Based on Acts 9:1-18

THEME: Look at the world through the eyes of love.

    I want to tell you a story about a man who did ugly, horrible things to people who loved and believed in Jesus. He was one of Jesus' worst enemies. His name was Paul. One day Paul was on his way to Damascus looking for Christians to arrest and put in chains, but on his way there, Jesus came down from heaven in a light that was so bright, it blinded Paul. All of you close your eyes for a minute. See how dark it is? That is what it was like for Paul. He couldn't see anything for three whole days. After the three days, Jesus sent a man to talk to Paul and to tell him that from now on, instead of arresting and hurting Christians, he was going to go about showing people how to become Christians.

    When Jesus took away Paul's sight, it was like he was shutting the door to all the ugly things Paul had done, and when he gave Paul back his sight, it was like opening the door to a new life and showing Paul the world through a new pair of eyes.

    Paul went on to lead thousands and thousands of people to

Jesus, and through his story and the letters he wrote that are in the Bible, he is still leading people to Jesus. You see, Jesus saw Paul's potential. POTENTIAL. Say that word for me — POTENTIAL. Potential means what you are capable of, and Jesus sees the potential in each one of you. When you use your potential for Jesus, it is like he gives you new eyes to look through so that you can see the world in a whole different way. He does that so you can see the world through the eyes of love.

Bible Verse:

The Bible verse today comes from **Acts 9:17**. You say after me: "**Paul, the Lord Jesus who appeared to you on the road, has sent me so that you may be filled with the Holy Spirit and get your sight back.**"

God gave us his son, Jesus, to carry with us in our hearts, and when we invite Jesus to live in our hearts, we see the world through a new pair of eyes, eyes that are filled with love. Close your eyes again and look at the darkness. Now open them, and look at all the beauty around you. The world of God around you is so beautiful, but even more beautiful is the world of God within you, and the only way to have that is through Jesus.

Sermon Ending:

I brought each of you a pair of glasses to help you remember how Paul learned to see the world through a new pair of eyes, eyes filled with the love of Jesus, and oh, what a difference that has made.

Devotional Ending:

Be like Paul, and learn to see the world through a new pair of eyes, eyes filled with the love of Jesus. Oh, what a difference that will make.

Prayer:

Now, bow your head, close your eyes, and let's talk to God. You say after me: "**Dear God, Help me to see the world through the eyes of love. Fill my heart with Jesus. Amen.**"

How To Talk To Children About God

(I gave the children plastic glasses with cardboard insets. There was a hole in the cardboard to see through. They came from the Oriental Trading Catalog Many dollar stores and toy stores have plastic fun glasses for children. Sun glasses would <u>not</u> be appropriate here.)

#53
The Problems Of Roads
Based on John 16:29-33

THEME: Put Jesus in your driver's seat.

I want to talk to you about the roads we take. The reason for a road is to help you get somewhere you are going. Some roads lead to big cities, some roads lead to little towns, while some roads lead to the ocean or a lake or just a little pond. Other roads take you to friend's houses. Those kinds of roads are the kind we drive on in cars.

There are other kinds of roads though. They are the roads of life. Some "life-roads" lead to happiness and good fortune, while some lead to trouble. No matter what kind of road you take, whether it is a road you drive on or a "life-road," you will run into problems sometimes along the way. Jesus even warns us about that in the Bible. He tells us that all of us are going to face problems and sadness, but he also tells us to cheer up because he will help us get through them.

Problems can make us sad. Hard times make some people bitter. But if it weren't for the feeling of SAD, we wouldn't be able to understand the feeling of HAPPY. If it weren't for hard times, we wouldn't be able to appreciate and enjoy good times. And if it weren't for problems, we wouldn't learn to cope or understand the gift of HELP.

Yes, the roads you take in life will have their problems, but understand that no problem is too big when you let Jesus help you through it.

Bible Verse:

The Bible verse today comes from **John 16:33**. You say after me: "**Here on earth you will have many trials and sorrows, but cheer up, for I have overcome the world.**"

William Hale White once wrote that some people find it hard to believe in Jesus — not because he is so far off — but because he is so close. Jesus is close, and he will travel down every road you take if you will just ask him to.

Sermon Ending:

I brought each of you a little car today to remind you to put Jesus in your driver's seat, and he will help you get down every road in your life, no matter what problems you encounter along the way.

Devotional Ending:

Always remember to put Jesus in your driver's seat, and he will get you down every road in your life, no matter what problems you encounter along the way.

Prayer:

Now, bow your head, close your eyes, and let's talk to God. You say after me: "**Dear God, Teach me to face all my problems with the help of Jesus. Amen.**"

(Little metal cars can be found in packets of 6 or more in most stores that carry toys.)

#54

Honorably Humble
Based on Luke 14:7-11

THEME: God will honor you for loving and helping others.

I want to talk to you about honor today. When someone treats you with honor, that means they treat you special. Have any of you ever been to a birthday party? Usually, when you go to a birthday party, it is because you like the person having the birthday, and you take them a present to show them you are glad they were born and happy that they are alive. You honor them for being a special friend. However, if the birthday person told you that you had to come to their party because they were better than everybody else, and you had to bring them a super, terrific present, and then they bragged and showed-off when you got there — well, you wouldn't feel like showing them honor. You see, honor is something you earn. It is not something you can demand.

Jesus thought honor was so important that he taught a specific lesson about it. Jesus does not want you to go around trying to make people honor you by being a show-off or by bragging about how important you are. He wants you to be gentle and kind. He wants you to be good to people who can't pay you back for it. God sees honor in that.

Bible Verse:

The Bible verse today comes from **Luke 14:11**. You say after me: **"For everyone who tries to honor himself shall be humbled; and he who humbles himself shall be honored."**

It is wonderful to receive honor from people, but what you need to strive for is honor from God. God will honor you for loving and helping others who can't pay you back.

Sermon Ending:

I brought each of you a little birthday cake today. I am honoring you because I am glad you were born, I am happy you are alive, and because you are learning to honor God by listening to the lessons of Jesus.

Devotional Endings:

I am glad you were born, I am happy you are alive, and I am proud of you for learning to honor God by listening to the lessons of Jesus.

Prayer:

Now, bow your head, close your eyes, and let's talk to God. You say after me: **"Dear God, Thank you for the lessons you sent to us through Jesus. Amen."**

(I made each child a little cake in a tin-foil potpie pan and decorated it. It was a bit larger than a cupcake and the foil pan made it more sturdy for the children to carry. I put cellophane over each cake and secured it with a rubber band.)

#55

One Kangaroo
Based on Genesis 3:9

THEME: You can't hide from God.

One of my favorite games as a child was "Hide and Seek" where someone would hide and the rest of the kids would try to find him or her. I remember when it was my turn to hide, the others would cover their eyes and count to ten, but to keep from counting too fast, we had a rule where you had to count out loud and say "KANGAROO" after each number — like this: 1 kangaroo, 2 kangaroo, 3 kangaroo, until you got to 10 kangaroo, and then you would shout, "Ready or not, here I come!"

I always tried to hide in a place where no one had hidden before because I didn't want to be found too easily, however, I most definitely wanted to be found. I didn't want to stay hidden all day, or I would have lost out on my turn to look for someone else. I would have missed out on playing with my friends. If I stayed hidden too long, I began to get lonesome and wish I hadn't hidden quite so well, and then I worried that the other kids would get tired of looking for me and quit. So, if I wasn't found after a short while, I would pop out of my hiding place and say, "Here I am!"

You know, you can hide from people, you can hide from your parents, but you can't hide from God. No matter where you go or what you do, God can see you before you can say 1 kangaroo.

Bible Verse:

The Bible verse today comes from **Genesis 3:9.** You say after me: **"The Lord called to Adam, 'Why are you hiding?'"**

Adam, the very first person God made, had done something wrong, and he was so ashamed that he wanted to hide from God. But God knew what Adam had done, and he knew where Adam was hiding.

There are things we all do that are wrong and cause us shame, and even if we hide the truth from other people, even if we hide ourselves from other people, we can't hide the truth or ourselves from God. Our wrongdoings sometimes cause others not to want to keep looking for us or keep playing with us, but thankfully, that is not the case with God. If we are sorry for what we've done wrong and ask God to forgive us — if we say, "Here I am," God will forgive us and love us and never stop.

Sermon Ending:

I brought each of you a kangaroo to help you remember that God doesn't play "Hide and Seek." You should seek God, but don't try to hide from God. He will find you before you can say 1 kangaroo.

Devotional Ending:

God doesn't play "Hide and Seek." You should seek God, but don't try to hide from God. He will find you before you can say 1 kangaroo.

Prayer:

Now, bow your head, close your eyes, and let's talk to God. You say after me: **"Dear God, Here I am! Please forgive me for all that I have done wrong. Amen."**

Goldfish and Silver Kisses

(I had one of my artistic students draw a pattern of a kangaroo head that could be glued to a popsicle craft stick. We made the kangaroos out of brown, black, and white construction paper.)

#56
The Color Of Truth
Based on Mark 7:1-8,14-15, 21-23

THEME: God looks for goodness, not just good works.

    I want to teach you a new word today. It is not a pretty word, and nobody likes to be called by this word. The word is HYPOCRITE. Say that for me. HYPOCRITE. A hypocrite is a person who pretends to love God but doesn't truly love God at all. Hypocrites do good works to make themselves look good in front of other people, and they like to tell people what good things they have done. Hypocrites are more concerned with what *people* think about them than what *God* thinks about them.

    You see, God appreciates people who give and don't tell God honors people who love without conditions. God looks at why you do good deeds as much as he looks at the good deeds you do.

    Some people think that if a Christian does anything bad or anything wrong, it makes him or her a hypocrite, and that is just not true. This church is full of Christians who have made mistakes and who have done things God didn't like. A Christian might even make as many mistakes as a hypocrite does, the difference is, a Christian truly wants God to forgive them and help them do better, and it doesn't occur to a hypocrite to care.

Bible Verse:

The Bible verse today comes from **Mark 7:23**. You say after me: **"Ugly things that come from within are what pollute you and make you unfit for God."**

Some people use the word hypocrite for an excuse not to come to church. They know they can't be or act perfect, and they are afraid others would call them a hypocrite if they went to church. They know they are unfit for God. The truth is, none of us are good enough to have this privilege of worshiping God in his church, but the rest of that truth is, God's grace and forgiveness gives us permission to come to his church. I can't think of a better place for imperfect people to gather than in God's house where we learn how to try and live a more Godly life.

Sermon Ending:

I brought each of you a chocolate crayon today. It is a reminder that truth is the color of goodness — not just good works. Truth is the color of God.

Devotional Ending:

Truth is the color of goodness — not just good works. Truth is the color of God.

Prayer:

Now, bow your head, close your eyes, and let's talk to God. You say after me: **"Dear God, Let truth and goodness spill from my heart and into the lives of others. Amen."**

(I found chocolate crayons at The World Market. A jumbo crayon for each child that can actually be colored with would also be a good choice. The Oriental Trading Catalog has all sorts of crayon items like crayon erasers, cups, banks and boxes of crayons that can be bought in units very reasonably.)

#57
Store My Treasures In Heaven
Based on Matthew 6:19-24

THEME: Store God's word in your heart, and you will be storing treasures in heaven.

Our lesson today comes from the scripture passage in Matthew where Jesus teaches about money, and do you know what Jesus says? Jesus says to store your treasures in heaven where they will never lose their value. I brought some things to show you in order to explain what it means for something to lose its value. *(The presenter needs to bring something they have around the house that is no longer valuable. It could be some old tennis shoes, or even old towels. If you have something that would be more fascinating to children, it would be better — something unusual or from a different era no longer used. I just happened to have a collection of old fur muffs that I bought off E-bay for an average of $7.00 a piece. Change the story to fit what you bring.)*

These are genuine fur muffs. Many years ago ladies and little girls would use them to keep their hands warm. These are very, very old, a couple of them about 100 years old, so be careful as you pass them around. If I were to buy a muff brand new, it would cost at least $600. I checked. But since these muffs are old, used, second hand, and outdated, I was able to buy them for around $7 a piece, even though they are still beautiful and warm and usable. You see, they lost their value over time.

Jesus was very wise and he knew that things — STUFF — would lose their value over time. He also knew what would never lose its value, and those are the things like love, faithfulness, praise for God, and God's word.

God has a plan for each one of you. I don't know what it is and right now you may not either, but if you continue to worship God and hold Jesus in your heart, God will guide you and lead you down the path he has chosen for you. Every time you follow God's direction, you are storing up real treasures in heaven that will never lose their value.

Bible Verse:

The Bible verse today comes from **Matthew 6:20**. You say after me: "**Store your treasures in heaven where they will never lose their value.**"

Sermon Ending:

I brought each of you something today that will never lose its value. It is God's word — a New Testament Bible. God's word has already outlasted the test of time. The cover may become worn and tattered some day, but the message inside never will. Store God's words in your heart, and you will be storing treasures in heaven.

Devotional Ending:

(Presenter should hold up a Bible.) This is something that will never lose its value. It is God's word. It is God's Bible. God's word has already outlasted the test of time. The cover may become worn and tattered some day, but the message inside never will. Store God's words in your heart, and you will be storing treasures in heaven.

Prayer:

Now, bow your head, close your eyes, and let's talk to God. You say after me: **"Dear God, Give me the desire to follow your lead and to know what is truly valuable. Amen."**

(I called the number listed in the phone directory for The Gideons. They were happy to let me have enough New Testaments for my church children. I think they will take donations, but they will not sell you their Bibles. What a wonderful organization!)

#58
Rocks And Cornerstones
Based on Matthew 2:33-43 and Isaiah 28:6

THEME: Build your life on the foundation of Jesus through prayer and commitment.

I want to talk to you about stones today. If you were to take a rock or a stone and throw it at someone, it could hurt them, even kill them. If a rock or a stone came falling down on your head, it could crush you and break all your bones. That is because rocks and stones are tough and sturdy and solid. A rock can withstand time, ages of time, and because of all those qualities, big buildings can be built on rocks.

Jesus is often compared to a rock or a stone because he is sturdy and solid and has withstood the test of time. He is often called the Cornerstone. The cornerstone of a building is its place of beginning, a place of honor in that building on which it rests solidly and steadfast. If we build our lives on Jesus, if we make him the cornerstone of our lives, he will stand steadfast for us and give us a solid foundation in love, in trust, in honor, and the promise that we can spend eternity with him in heaven. Jesus wants to be the cornerstone in our lives. He wants us to get to know him, love him, and trust him.

You know how the more you talk to someone, the better you get to know them and the more comfortable you feel around them? It's like that with Jesus. When you pray to God, you are talking to Jesus at the same time, and he is listening to every single word you say. Before you know it, he has crawled right inside your heart and become the cornerstone of your life.

When you pray, it doesn't have to be fancy. Just speak what is in your heart and be honest. I have a book titled *Children's Letters to God*. It is full of prayers, honest heartfelt prayers, from kids your ages. Maybe it will show you that you can talk to God or Jesus about anything. *(I read some prayers from that book, ISBN number 0-89480-999-7. If you cannot get that book, then ask a Sunday school teacher or a teacher from an elementary school, who teaches first grade or kindergarten, to have their students write down a prayer to God for you. Then select a few to read for this lesson.)*

Bible Verse:

The Bible verse today comes from **Isaiah 28:6**. You say after me: **"God says, I am placing a Foundation Stone in Zion — a firm, tested, precious cornerstone that is safe to build on."**

God is talking about Jesus — the Cornerstone. Build your lives on that cornerstone. Build on it day by day through prayer and commitment to Jesus.

Sermon Ending:

I brought each of you a pad of paper today so you can write down or draw things you need to talk to Jesus about. When you have your pad filled up, you will be surprised at how much closer you are to Jesus.

Devotional Ending:

The more you pray, the closer you will become to Jesus.

Prayer:

Now, bow your head, close your eyes, and let's talk to God.

You say after me: "**Dear God, I want Jesus to be the cornerstone of my life. Amen.**"

(The Oriental Trading Catalog *has little notepads with religious covers. Notepads with assorted decorative covers can be bought in bundles at dollar stores. Betty, thanks for the book,* Children's Letters to God.*)*

#59
Simply Believe
Based on Mark 10:13-16 and Matthew 18:1-6

THEME: Always keep your "childlike" faith in God.
Did you know that Jesus thinks you are special? Jesus thinks children are so special that he told his disciples on more than one occasion that he wanted them to be more like children. Jesus didn't want his disciples to act childish, but he wanted them to be *childlike* in their faith and belief. Let me explain by telling you what the Bible says in the book of Matthew, chapter 18. It says the disciples came to Jesus to ask which of them would be greatest in the Kingdom of Heaven. Jesus called a small child over to him and set the little fellow down among them and said, "Unless you turn to God from your sins and become as little children, you will never get into the Kingdom of Heaven. Therefore anyone who humbles himself as this little child, is the greatest in the Kingdom of Heaven."

Jesus was saying that little children don't worry about which people are going to be most important in this world or in heaven. They *simply* believe God is most important. They *simply* trust and believe in God.

As you grow up, you will learn that there are some people you can't trust, but always trust in Jesus, in God, and in the Holy Spirit. Never let anyone take the belief you have in God now and weaken that. Hold on to it with all your might. Guard it with all that is in you. Help it to grow by listening to Bible stories and by learning to read and study the Bible on your own. Share your trust and belief in God with those who have lost theirs. Help them find it by talking to them about Jesus.

Bible Verse:

The Bible verse today comes from **Mark 10:14**. You say after me: **"Jesus said, 'Let the children come to me, for the Kingdom of God belongs to such as them.'"**

(The following is from the song, "Jesus Loves Me," but instead of singing it, speak it with meaning to the children, replacing the word "me" with "you.") Jesus loves you, this I know, for the Bible tells me so. Little ones to him belong. They are weak, but he is strong. Yes, Jesus loves you. Yes, Jesus loves you. Yes, Jesus loves you. The Bible tells me so.

Sermon Ending:

I brought each of you a glow in the dark bouncing ball that says, "Smile, Jesus loves you." It is to help you remember to always keep your resilient and bouncy childlike faith in God, and know without question that Jesus loves YOU.

Devotional Ending:

Always keep your childlike faith in God, and know without question that Jesus loves YOU.

Prayer:

Now, bow your head, close your eyes, and let's talk to God. You say after me: **"Dear God, Thank you for the faith you planted in me. Help me keep it forever childlike. Amen."**

(These balls are in the Oriental Trading Catalog *as well as several other varieties of "Jesus loves you" items in the religious section.)*

#60

I'm In A Fix
Based on Philippians 4:6

THEME: Look at your own faults before you look for faults in others.

Would you like to know what one of my problems is? I have a tendency to want to tell God what to do. I'll ask him for guidance and help, then turn right around and tell him where to lead me and how to do it. I'll tell you another problem I have. If I let someone upset me or irritate me, I'm bad about praying for them as if something is wrong with them, and God needs to fix them.

Just the other day at work, another teacher made a statement that I didn't agree with. I heard myself praying inside my head, "God, do something with her, please. She is "thowed off." "Thowed off" is an expression used by prison inmates that means crazy. Now tell me, how ugly and arrogant was I to think it my place to tell God what's wrong with somebody else just because I disagreed with something they said? I've thought about it and decided it was very ugly and that if I'm going to pray, I need to do it with a loving and nonjudgmental heart. You see, I

realized that it was myself I needed to be praying about and my attitude toward that teacher. I needed to get my heart right.
Bible Verse:
The Bible verse today comes from **Matthew 5:8**. You say after me: "**Blessed are the pure in heart for they shall see God.**"

Praying is talking to God. When we pray about someone, we are talking to God about someone he loves and created. I'm trying to learn how to pray by not asking for God to change others, but for God to change my attitude about others and create in me a pure heart. There is a peace that comes in letting God decide who needs fixing and when. I am discovering that more often than not, it's me that needs fixing.
Sermon Ending:
In case you ever have problems like mine, I brought each of you a mirror. The next time you want God to fix somebody, look in the mirror and ask instead for God to check and see if you need fixing first.
Devotional Ending:
The next time you want God to fix somebody, look in a mirror and ask instead for God to check and see if you need fixing first.
Prayer:
Now, bow your head, close your eyes, and let's talk to God. You say after me: "**Dear God, Help me see my own faults before I notice them in others. Create in me a pure heart. Amen.**"

(Little mirrors come several to a package at dollar stores.)

#61
Spouse Alert
Based on Psalms 32:8

THEME: Ask God to put the right people in your life.

I find it so comforting that I can pray to God. Don't you? The Bible tells us that God hears our prayers and will answer our prayers if we choose to let him. The key point here is — if we let HIM. Of course that means we won't always get our way. You see, God knows a lot more than we do, and I have discovered that God makes the best choice when we leave the choice up to him.

God answers prayers. The problems come when we don't bother to pray, and especially when we don't pray about the important things. For example, you might pray for a new bike or a new puppy or a bigger allowance. You might even pray for a trip to Disney Land, but we often don't think to pray for the things that will affect our lives the most.

I want to give you some advice today about something to start praying about now, at your age. I want you to start praying that God will find for you the right person to marry when you are grown. I want you to do that because the person you marry, if you choose to ever get married, has such a huge impact on your life, and if you leave that choice up to God, he will choose the right person for you and arrange for you to meet. Perhaps that sounds extraordinary, supernatural, magical, and miraculous, but then that is exactly what God is. All of the above.

Bible Verse:

The Bible verse today comes from **Psalms 32:8**. You say after me: **"I will instruct you and teach you in the way you should go. I will guide you with my eyes."**

Ask any Christian and they will tell you how powerful and almighty God is, but there are times we Christians fail to allow God to work his almighty power in our lives. It's as though we don't really believe God will do what he said he would do. Remember this: It is so important that you really BELIEVE in God if you are going to believe in God at all.

Sermon Ending:

I brought each of you a prayer tablet in the shape of a cross. Write down or draw things in this prayer journal that you need to pray about. Put down the important things, and ask God to guide you in your choices.

Devotional Ending:

Start keeping a prayer journal. Write down or draw things in you prayer journal that you need to pray about. Put down the important things, and ask God to guide you in your choices.

Prayer:

Now, bow your head, close your eyes, and let's talk to God. You say after me: **"Dear God, In your extraordinary way, guide me to make wise choices. Amen."**

(The cross-shaped tablets are available in the Oriental Trading Catalog.*)*

#62
Human Nature
Based on Romans 4:23-5:11

THEME: Jesus gave you the honor of becoming God's child.

Our Bible verse today comes from the book of Romans. I want us to say it at the beginning of our lesson today.
Bible Verse:

It is from **Romans 5:11**. You say after me: "**Now we rejoice in our wonderful new relationship with God — all because of what our Lord Jesus Christ has done in dying for our sins — making us friends with God.**"

From the very beginning, God wanted to be a friend to the people he put on earth, and it could have been that way, but God chose to give people free will. In other words he gave us a human nature, the ability to make our own choices and decisions about things, and that is when the trouble started. You see, it is human nature to be bad sometimes. Since people made bad choices so often, they weren't holy enough to have a personal relationship with God. People weren't good enough to be God's friends, and it made God sad, so God gave us a way to become his personal friend. God decided to come to earth as a man, but he wanted to be born with a human nature so people could have a better understanding of him. Through his own miracle, God sent a part of himself to earth and was born as a human baby — a baby named Jesus. In this way, God remained our Lord and Creator, and at the same time became our Lord and Savior through Jesus, the man he called his only begotten son.

Jesus grew up as a person with a human nature, but even before he knew he was the Son of God, Jesus displayed a Godly nature. He always made the right choices. He was never ugly or bad. He was pure goodness even though he was faced with all the same temptations and desires we are.

It wasn't long ago when I truly understood why Jesus suffered so when he was crucified. Oh, I knew that being nailed to a cross had to have been horrible, but that is not what hurt Jesus so. What hurt Jesus most was that he took all the ugliness and sinfulness and badness of mankind onto himself to take it away from us. Jesus was pure goodness, and for the sake of mankind, he swallowed up all our ugliness just so we could be friends of God — so we could become God's children too. And that is why we call him Savior.

Sermon Ending:

I brought you a medal today emblazoned with a cross to remind you that Jesus, by taking on your sinful nature at the cross, gave you the honor of becoming God's friend — God's child.

Devotional Ending:

Always remember that when Jesus took on your sinful nature at the cross, he gave you the honor of becoming God's friend, God's child.

Prayer:

Now, bow your head, close your eyes, and let's talk to Jesus. You say after me: **"Dear Jesus, Thank you for how you gave me** the honor of being God's friend and God's child. Amen."

(The Oriental Trading Catalog *has these medals and they come on a red, white, and blue ribbon for the children to wear around their necks.)*

#63

I'm Sure!
Based on Hebrews 11:1

THEME: Your faith in God shouldn't change with the situation.

I want to talk to you about faith and hope today. Faith begins by believing that God is who he says he is. When you can believe that, you can believe God's promises. When you can believe God's promises, hope becomes the force that drives you forward into each new day.

Hope can be the difference between a person being good or a person being bad. You see, a person who is good, has hope for good things to come. A person who is bad, doesn't believe good things will happen. Sometimes a person will act good in one situation and act bad in another situation. One of the things we all need to learn and understand is that our faith in God should not change with our situation.

When things aren't going our way, when we are hurt or sick, or in bad trouble, we must hope for better days ahead and cling to our faith that God will give us an understanding of our hard

times and always walk beside us.
Bible Verse:

The Bible verse today comes from **Hebrews 11:1.** You say after me: **"Now faith is being sure of what we hope for and certain of what we do not see."**

There is something God wants us to do in order to make hope and faith real in our lives. He wants us to do all that we can to help ourselves and others. He wants us to work for good, be the best that we can be, and try to make what has gone wrong become right. And when we have done all we can and we get to the end our rope — well, God is there waiting to help. It is there that we must learn to stand on our faith that God will carry us through.

Sermon Ending:

I brought each of you a little dove pin to wear. A dove is a symbol of faith. Let hope and faith in God be your strength.

Devotional Ending:

Let hope and faith in God be your strength. God will carry you through.

Prayer:

Now, bow your head, close your eyes, and let's talk to God. You say after me: **"Dear God, Help me see with my heart that which I cannot see with my eyes. Amen."**

(Little dove pins are available in the Oriental Trading Catalog.*)*

#64
Clothed
Based on Colossians 3:12

THEME: Clothe yourself in the goodness of Jesus.

I want to talk to you about clothes today. Clothes are something you wear to keep from being seen in your birthday suit. Clothes are something you wear for protection from the outside elements like the sun or the cold or bugs. The clothes you wear can show others a little bit about what kind of person you are: athletic, business-like, creative, silly, or someone who marches to the beat of a different drummer (in other words — unusual).

Yes, clothes can tell a lot about a person, but the kind of clothes I want to tell you about today aren't the kind you wear on the outside of your body, they are the kind you wear on the inside. The clothes I'm talking about are explained in the Bible in the book of Colossians, and that is where our Bible verse come from today.

Bible Verse:

The Bible verse comes from **Colossians 3:12**. You say after me: **"Clothe yourselves with compassion, kindness, humility,**

gentleness and patience."

When we wear compassion, it means that we feel sorry for someone who is going through a hard time, and we want to make things better for them. When we wear kindness, it means we are helpful and good toward others. When we wear humility, it means we do our best to be good and not show off about it. When we wear gentleness, it means we are careful with others' feelings. And when we wear patience, it means we are understanding and not in a hurry to get mad at others.

When you wear all these clothes — compassion, kindness, humility, gentleness and patience, it means you are clothed with Jesus, and others will see him in you. There is no clothing on earth more beautiful than that.

Sermon Ending:

I brought each of you two Hawaiian leis today because they stand for friendship and good feelings. Keep one as a reminder to clothe yourself in the good things we talked about today. Give the other one away as a symbol of your willingness to show love and kindness toward others.

Devotional Ending:

Dress yourself with Jesus everyday.

Prayer:

Now, bow your head, close your eyes, and let's talk to God. You say after me: **"Dear God, Clothe me with the goodness of Jesus. Amen."**

(Hawaiian leis can be found at party stores and in the Oriental Trading Catalog.*)*

#65
Look Through The Eyes Of Faith
Based on Matthew 18:10-11

THEME: God has blessed you with your own angel.

I want everybody to take a deep breath and let it out. *(Presenter should demonstrate this.)* When you breathe, what is it that you take into your lungs through your mouth and nose? It's air. That's right. Can you see air? No. Grab some air and hold it in your hands. Can you? No, you can't hold air in your hands. Sometimes you can feel air, like when the wind blows.

Speaking of wind — in my yard I have some very big, very tall trees. *(If you live in an area where there are no trees, just use something else that is manipulated by the wind and change the story to match that, or show a picture of some trees being blown in a hurricane for example.)* I can walk up to one of those trees and push as hard as I can, but no matter how hard I try, I can't push one over. But something that is invisible, something I can't grab hold of, something that I can breathe into my lungs, can be strong enough to push one of those huge trees over. AIR!

I want you to be very still and listen for a second. Can you hear any air right now? No. Just because we aren't able to see something or touch it or hear it, doesn't always mean that it is not there — like angels for example. Angels are spiritual beings, created by God, who carry out his work on earth. Angels are spirit messengers sent out to help and care for us. Angels serve people and protect people, and the Bible says that each one of you has angels assigned to you, watching over you for God. You may not be able to see them or touch them or hear them, but they are there. The Bible says they are.

The Bible says we are never to pray to angels or worship angels, but we need to be aware of them. Angels are special blessings from God, and we should be mindful that they are around.

I want to do an experiment for you. I want to try to make it possible for you to see air. *(Presenter needs to have some dry ice in a bowl. Pour some water over the dry ice.)* When something is visible, it is easy to believe it is there.

Bible Verse:

The Bible verse comes from **Matthew 18:10**. You say after me: **"Don't look down upon little children. For in heaven their angels have constant access to God."**

Sermon Ending:

Angels are spirits that you cannot touch or see perhaps, but you need to have faith that they are around. FAITH is believing in something you cannot see or hear or hold in your hand. I cannot produce an angel for you or make one show up like I did the air, but I have a little angel for you to carry in your pocket or purse. It's to remind you how special you are to God, so special that he has blessed you with your own angels.

Devotional Ending:

Angels are spirits that you cannot touch or see perhaps, but you need to have faith that they are around. FAITH is believing in something you cannot see or hear or hold in your hand. I cannot produce an angel for you or make one show up like I did the air, but don't be surprised if at times you sense one in your presence.

Prayer:

Now, bow your head, close your eyes, and let's talk to God. You say after me: "**Dear God, Thank you for my angels. Make my faith strong. Amen.**"

(I bought little plastic angels, about an inch tall each, in a craft store. You could make an angel out of any number of things and disregard the part about carrying it in their pocket.)

#66

Spend Promises Wisely
Based on Genesis 9:8-17
(God's Rainbow)

THEME: Take promises seriously; make promises seriously.

I want to talk about promises today. Perhaps some of you have said something like: "I promise I'll eat my lunch if you'll just let me have one more cookie," or "I promise I won't be fussy about getting out of bed in the morning if you'll just let me finish watching this TV show," or "Please let me go with you. I promise I'll be good." Did you keep your promise every time? You know, a promise is a very valuable thing, and it must be spent that way.

Promises aren't something to make lightly or throw away. When you make a promise, it means that you will try your very best to do what you said you would do unless it means that you or someone else could get hurt.

Sometimes promises are sealed with symbols. Take a wedding ring for example. When my husband *(spouse, wife, or use "a husband," etc.)* placed this ring on my finger at our wedding, he promised to love, honor, and cherish me until one of us died. This ring is the symbol of his promise, and because this ring represents his promise to love me, it is my most favorite and treasured *thing* that I own. Wearing it makes me feel special.

Let me tell you about another symbol or sign for a very special promise. Do you remember the story about Noah and the ark? Noah built a great big boat, called an ark, and he put his family and two of every kind of animal on it because God was going to flood the earth. Well, God did flood the earth, and every living thing on earth died that wasn't on that boat.

You see, the people down here on earth were out of control. They were evil, vicious, and wicked, and they had no intentions of changing. The Bible said it broke God's heart. God wiped them out! They all drowned except Noah and his family and those animals on the ark.

After the flood was over and the earth dried out, God made a promise. He promised to never again destroy the earth with a flood. Like when my husband gave me this wedding ring to seal his promise, God gave us something to seal the promise he made.

I want to read to you from my Bible what God said. *Genesis: 9:11-13 "I solemnly promise you and your children and the animals you brought with you — all these birds and cattle and wild animals — that I will never again send another flood to destroy the earth. And I seal this promise with this sign: I have placed my rainbow in the clouds as a sign of my promise until the end of time, to you and to all the earth."*

Every time I see a rainbow, I feel special. That rainbow is a gift to me from God, and I treasure that gift. It *means* something to me.

Bible Verse:

The Bible verse today comes from **Genesis 9:13.** You say after me: **"I have placed my rainbow in the clouds as a sign of my promise."**

Take promises seriously, and more importantly, make promises seriously. Follow God's example and keep the promises you make.

Sermon Ending:

I have a rainbow for you to make like this one. *(See notes below.)* As you create your rainbow, remember that a rainbow is a symbol of a promise from God, and the next time you see a real one, stop and realize that it is a gift to you from God — a symbol of his promise.

Devotional Ending:

Remember that a rainbow is a symbol of a promise from God, and the next time you see a real one, stop and realize that it is a gift to you from God — a symbol of his promise.

Prayer:

Now, bow your head, close your eyes, and let's talk to God. You say after me: **"Dear God, Thank you for keeping your promise. Help me to keep my promises. Amen."**

(I used the rainbow idea from the book "Bible Fun for Everyone." See my introduction on how to find this book. I included all the pieces to make the project and put them in individual ziplock bags for the children. At the Dollar Tree I just happened to find a large gift bag with Noah's Ark and a rainbow on it. Across the top was written **"God's Promise."** *I used it to carry the individual rainbow projects in. God will show you things like the rainbow bag too if you are open to his help. He will actually guide you to the perfect item to help bring your lesson across to his little children. Remember, they are HIS little children. Did you read my introduction?)*

#67
Sadness Or Gladness
Based on Psalms 118:24

THEME: Be glad for what you have.

Have you ever exaggerated? That is a stuffed word, isn't it? EXAGGERATED. It means to enlarge beyond the truth — in other words, make something sound bigger than it really is. For example: I would be exaggerating if I said, "I caught a fish this big," *(presenter should stretch out their arms real wide)* and it really was only this big. *(With hands show a more average fish size.)* I wanted to talk about that word to explain how some people get so sad and stay that way.

Things happen in life that make people truly sad, but even when a person is as sad as they have ever been, it is important to look for something to be glad about. Often we let sadness become exaggerated, bigger than it should be, and before you know it, sadness can swallow all your gladness and leave you empty. When that happens to a person, they lose touch with God, and when a person loses touch with God, the devil tries to creep in.

There is a way to keep that from happening. You must keep God in front of you, so he can lead you. You must keep God behind you so he can guide you, and you must keep God beside you to keep you in-line with what is true and real. And what is true and real is God's unending love for you.

Bible Verse:

The Bible verse today comes from **Psalms 118:24**. You say after me: **"This is the day the Lord has made; let us rejoice and be glad in it."**

George Bernard Shaw once wrote, "People exaggerate the value of things they haven't got." That means that sometimes people think, if I only had this or that, I'd be happy, but then when they get it, the happiness doesn't last. That is why it is so important to find happiness in what God has given you — like each new day, the air you breathe, the song of a bird, or the stars in the sky.

It is normal to want things and even to become disappointed when you don't get them.

Just remember to not let things be what you place your value in. Place your value in God's love and in each new day that he gives you to explore, and be glad in it.

Sermon Ending:

I brought each of you a key ring with a sun, moon, or star on it. Let it remind you that the key to happiness is finding value in what you have — not in what you don't have. You have all the magic of God wrapped in each night and day. Treasure it and be glad in it.

Devotional Ending:

The key to happiness is finding value in what you have — not in what you don't have. You have all the magic of God wrapped in each night and day. Treasure it and be glad in it.

Prayer:

Now, bow your head, close your eyes, and let's talk to God.

You say after me: "**Dear God, Help me find value in what I have. Fill my heart with gladness. Amen.**"

(The celestial key rings are in the Oriental Trading Catalog.*)*

#68
Standing On Standard
Based on I Samuel 16:17

THEME: Measure your standards by God's, not man's.

    The other day I saw a young woman who looked to be about twenty years old coming out of a prison gate. She had on a gray uniform, so I know she worked in the prison as a security officer. She was one of the prettiest young women I had ever seen. She was much smaller than the men she was walking out with, but she carried her shoulders back and her head high as though she felt ten feet tall. She had beautiful natural blonde hair pulled back in a pony tail, and her sweet young face made you think of angels. I thought, how wonderful it must feel to be that pretty, and then she spoke. The words that came out of her mouth were some of the filthiest, crude, ugly, and offensive words I have ever heard. I turned to look at her, and as I watched her talk, it was as though her beauty melted like ice cream on a hot summer afternoon. She no longer made me think of angels.

    I had assumed she was as sweet as an angel because of the way she looked on the outside, and then she showed me her character. People often judge others by the way they look. We look at models in magazines or watch movie stars on the movie screen and think, *I wish I could be just like him or her*, when in fact, we don't really know anything about their character — the way they act in real life, how they treat others, or whether or not they love God.

Bible Verse:
The Bible verse today comes from **I Samuel 16:7**. You say after me: **"Men judge by outward appearance, but the Lord looks at a person's thoughts and intentions."**

I think that young prison guard was trying to fit in, so she was trying to talk like some of the prisoners do. She probably thought that talking ugly would make the prisoners and other guards think she was tough. What she didn't realize was that talking ugly doesn't make you tough, it just makes you ugly. Strong character, good morals and God are what gives you the ability to handle tough situations.

Measure your standards of living, the way you act, by God's, not by man's. When you are around people who are acting and talking ugly, don't lower you standards to meet theirs. Keep your standards high, and just perhaps others around you will want to raise their standards to meet yours.

Sermon Ending:
I brought each of you a ruler today because a ruler is a tool we use to measure with. Let it remind you to measure your standards, your behavior, by God's. Let God be your ruler in more ways than one.

Devotional Ending:
Let God be your ruler in more ways than one. *(Presenter should hold up a ruler here.)*

Prayer:
Now, bow your head, close your eyes, and let's talk to God. You say after me: **"Dear God, Lift my standards high so others**

might see angels in me. Amen."

(Any ruler will do. Bright and colorful plastic ones that they could use in school would be a good idea.)

#69

God In Front — Jesus Inside
Based on Proverbs 3:6

THEME: Put God first in everything you do.

I want to talk to you about what it means to be a Christian. The word "Christ" is in the word Christian. *(Presenter should show a flash-card with the word Christian on it. The word Christ needs to be underlined.)* The word Christ means Messiah and Messiah means Savior — the deliverer who came to save us from hell and guide us to heaven.

A Christian is a person who believes that Jesus was and is Christ. A Christian loves Jesus and has asked him to live in his heart and be the Lord, the King, the Leader of his life. A true Christian tries to act in a way, talk in a way, and live in a way that Jesus would want him to.

When a Christian gets into a situation where he has to decide what to do, he should make his decision by asking himself, "What would Jesus do?"

Bible Verse:

The Bible verse today comes from **Proverbs 3:6.** You say after me: **"In everything you do, put God first, and he will direct you and crown your efforts with success."**

Putting God first by living for Jesus, is not always easy. It is hard to always say and do and feel the right thing. We Christians make wrong choices everyday, but what saves us and sets us apart from those who aren't Christians, is our love for Jesus and our belief that he died for our sins. Also, we ask for God's forgiveness, and we try to live right.

God asks that we never deny our love for Jesus or pretend that we are not Christians. You see, if you can't be a Christian everywhere, you can't truly be a Christian anywhere.

Sermon Ending:

I brought you a crown today to help you remember our Bible verse where God says he will crown our efforts with success if we put him first in everything we do. To put God first, you must invite Jesus to live in your heart so that you will truly know and understand God's love for you, and the plan he has for your life.

Devotional Ending:

Remember our Bible verse where God says he will crown our efforts with success if we put him first in everything we do. To put God first, you must invite Jesus to live in your heart so that you will truly know and understand God's love for you and the plan he has for your life.

Prayer:

Now, bow your head, close your eyes, and let's talk to God. You say after me: **"Dear God, I give Jesus my love. Thank you for giving Jesus to me. Amen."**

Go forth, little Christians, and make Jesus your crowning glory, and make God first in your life.

(I used little paper crowns I found at the Dollar Tree. However, you can find them at party stores or in the Oriental Trading Catalog.*)*

#70

Looking For Joy
Based on Proverbs 17:22

THEME: You will be as happy or sad as you choose to be.

Did you know that God wants you to be happy? He wants your heart to be full of joy, but some people don't know how to be happy. Those people tend to look for the bad in something instead of the good. They get into the habit of being sad, and before long, they don't even know where to look for joy.

You can find joy in the face of a friend. You can find happiness in the sound of music. Joy can come from holding a puppy or even seeing a picture of one in a book. Joy and happiness are everywhere you look if you *choose* to find it there, but it is just as easy to see sadness and misery in the very same places. It all depends on what you choose to see.

Take this rose for example. *(Presenter will need to hold up a real rose with thorns on it.)* I can look at it and see the thorns and think, if I touch this rose it could prick my finger, cause me pain, and make me bleed. Or I can look at the beautiful blossom and think, if I touch the petals, it will feel softer than velvet, and if I put it up to my nose, it will smell wonderful. This rose can offer pain or joy, depending on how you look at it and what you choose to see.

The next time you look up at heaven and see dark grey clouds with lightning streaking across them, what will you choose to see? Will it be the threat of a storm and a ruined afternoon, or will you see that God is graciously about to water our earth and cool the air for just a while? Hopefully you will watch the lightning from a window and think about how powerful God is.

Bible Verse:

The Bible verse today comes from **Proverbs 17:22**. You say after me: **"A cheerful heart does like good medicine; but a broken spirit makes one sick."**

God made the rose, God made the clouds and God made lightning. In all those things you can choose to see joy or you can choose to see sadness. What you have to realize is the joy nor the sadness is in any thing, the joy or the sadness comes from *inside* you. All you have to do is decide which one you want to pull out. You will be as happy or as sad as you make up your mind to be.

Sermon Ending:

I brought each of you a glow-in-the-dark smile face. It is to help you learn that a smile can bring out joy, and joy can bring a light to the dark. Choose to find joy; you don't have to look very far. It is right inside of you.

Devotional Ending:

A smile can bring out joy, and joy can bring a light to the dark. Choose to find joy. You don't have to look very far. It is right inside of you.

Prayer:

Now, bow your head, close your eyes, and let's talk to God. You say after me: **"Dear God, Give me a cheerful heart so that I can experience the joy of life. Amen."**

(The glow-in-the-dark smile faces can be found in the Oriental Trading Catalog.*)*

#71

Love Your Neighbor
*Based on Luke 10:25-37
(about the good Samaritan)*

THEME: Be kind to all your neighbors — even the ones you don't like.

Have you ever met somebody you didn't like? Maybe they talked too loud or too much, or with a different accent. Perhaps they were too big or too little. Maybe you didn't like them because they had ugly habits. Have you ever disliked someone because they dressed weird? I saw a girl the other day with purple and green hair. Some people are disliked because they are a different color and have different ways of doing things.

If you have met someone you didn't like, you are not alone. I would be willing to say that everyone in this church/place has met someone they didn't like. Jesus wants us to love everyone and offer our help if they need it, even if we don't like them and even if we disagree with how they act and live.

The Bible tells us in the book of Luke that one day a lawyer went to Jesus and asked him how a person could live forever in heaven. Jesus said, "Well you're a lawyer, what does God's law say?" The lawyer said, "You have to love God with all your heart, soul, strength, and mind. And you have to love your neighbor as much as you love yourself." Jesus said, "That's right!" But, the lawyer didn't want to love everyone so he said, "Well, which neighbors exactly do I have to love?"

Jesus answered him by telling this story: There was a Jewish man walking down the road. Some thieves saw him, beat him up, took his clothes, stole his money and left him lying there naked to die. A Jewish priest came by, saw him, crossed to the other side of the road; he didn't stop. Another Jewish religious leader came by, stopped and looked at him, but kept on going. After a while a Samaritan came along. Jews didn't like Samaritans because they were a mixed race of people and acted different than Jews, but the Samaritan stopped and helped the wounded man. He doctored him, carried him to an inn on his donkey, took care of him all night and gave the innkeeper enough money to care for him until he was well.

Jesus asked the lawyer, "Which of those three men was a good neighbor to the wounded man?" The lawyer said, "The Samaritan, even though Jews and Samaritans didn't like each other." Jesus said, "Yes. Now go and be like the good Samaritan."

It is okay not to like everybody. It is okay not to agree with everybody, but even if we don't like someone, Jesus wants us to show them love, help, and kindness when they need it.
Bible Verse:
The Bible verse today comes form **Luke 10:27**. You say after me: "**. . . love your neighbor just as much as you love yourself.**"
Sermon Ending:
I brought each of you a "Good Samaritan" bracelet. On the bracelet it has **WWJD**, which stands for "What would Jesus do?" That's to remind you to be loving, kind, and helpful to all your neighbors, even the ones you don't like very much.

Devotional Ending:
Always try to be loving, kind, and helpful to all your neighbors, even the ones you don't like very much.

Prayer:
Now, bow your head, close your eyes, and let's talk to God. You say after me: **"Dear God, Help us to be like the good Samaritan. Help us to love others. Amen."**

(The bracelets are canvas-type friendship bracelets and can be found in packages. Look where party favors are found. Dollar stores are great places to find such items. Friendship bracelets can also be purchased in the Oriental Trading Catalog *You could easily print WWJD on each bracelet with a Sharpie if you can't find them already printed.)*

#72

Holy Communion
Based on Matthew 26:26-29

THEME: Taking Communion is one the most special things we get to do as Christians.

I have something very serious to talk to you about. You will have to listen carefully so you will understand it. Will you do that? You see, there is something you need to know about God. Are you ready to know what it is? **God is absolutely, positively, and completely holy.** Back in time before Jesus came, people may have had more respect for God's holiness than people do now because they had to work at being forgiven by God for the things they did wrong — their sins.

In the Old Testament it tells us that God judged sin as being punishable by death. Think about it. Death! But God allowed people to try and work their way into being forgiven for their sins. Here is what they had to do: They had to find a certain kind of animal with no defects and no blemishes; nothing could be wrong with it. It couldn't even have a bug bite on it. They would kill this animal and offer it to God, and that would take the place of having to die themselves. The animal's blood was proof that one life had been given for another.

The shedding and spilling of blood was the price that had to be paid if a person was to become right with God. But we don't have to do that anymore because of one thing that happened. God allowed his son, Jesus, to die in our place so we will never again have to offer sacrifices for the things we do wrong. There is something we do in this church to help us keep sight of what Jesus did for us, and how he saved us from our sin. It is such an easy thing to do that perhaps we don't give it the honor and respect it deserves. It is called Communion. That is where we eat a piece of bread and drink a sip of wine. Taking Communion is an honor and privilege because of what it means. The bread symbolizes the body of Jesus. It is a way for us to take a part of Jesus' body into our bodies. The wine symbolizes his blood. It represents his life that we are drinking in to be a part of us.

Taking Communion is one of the most special things we get to do as Christians. It is a practice we follow to honor Jesus, to honor God, and to honor the forgiveness that was given to us through the death of Jesus on the cross.

Bible Verse:

The Bible verse today comes from **Matthew 26:28**. You say after me: **"This is my blood. It is poured out to forgive the sins of the multitudes."**

When Jesus died on the cross for us, his death made you and me acceptable in God's eyes. We have all sinned. We can't be or act good enough to get into heaven. Our ticket into heaven is through the blood of Jesus Christ, our Savior.

Sermon Ending:

I brought each of you a loaf of bread and a box of grape juice to take home to remind you of the two things we partake of during Communion. If you get to take Communion with us today, think seriously about what it means and what a privilege it is to be a part of.

Devotional Ending:

If you get to take Communion with us today, think seriously about what it means and what a privilege it is to be a part of.

Prayer:

Now, bow your head, close your eyes, and let's talk to God. You say after me: **"Dear God, Help me to understand and honor the sacrifice Jesus made for me. Amen."**

(I bought packages of little pre-cooked rolls and small individual containers of grape juice and put both in one zip-lock bag for each child.)

#73
The Lifetime Bath
Based on Luke 3:7-22
(baptism)

THEME: Don't take the love of God for granted.

I want to talk to you today about something that is very valuable, but it doesn't cost very much. Sometimes you can get it for free. I have seen it fall out of the sky. It is something you could not live without. It has no color and no taste in its purest form, and it has lots and lots of uses. People need it, animals need it, fish need it; even plants need it! You can play in it, cook with it, swim in it, bathe in it, and even drink it. What am I describing? WATER! Water is a wonderful substance. You need it to get you clean on the outside, and you need to drink water to cleanse you on the inside.

I want to tell you about another use for water. It is a symbolic use that stands for something very important. It is called baptism. Some of you have been baptized. In churches the pastor either sprinkles water over you, pours water over you, or dips you under water for a brief second. When that is done, we believe that God is washing away your sins. It is a way to display on the outside what is happening on the inside.

When we get dirt on our hands and body, we bathe and wash it off with water, but when we act dirty, we need God to wash that away. By being baptized, we show God that we want him to help us live right, and we want him to clean away our ugliness when we mess up. God doesn't ask us to be baptized every time we sin. Just doing it once is enough for him. God's bath lasts for a lifetime. I'll bet some of you little boys wish a regular bath would too.

Bible Verse:

The Bible verse today comes from **Luke 3:21**. You say after me: **"One day after the crowds had been baptized, Jesus himself was baptized."**

Jesus had no dirt in his heart; he was without sin, but he wanted to be baptized as an example to others that God will love you and forgive you and cleanse you if you love him and try to live for him.

Sermon Ending:

I brought each of you a bottle of water today. It is nothing special, but then again, it is very special. Water is something that we take for granted because it is so easy to come by. Sometimes we are that way by God. God is so easy to claim and receive that we take him for granted. After today, look at water in a different way. Love it, respect it, be thankful for it, and then remember to love God, respect God, and be thankful for him.

Devotional Ending:

You might think water is nothing special, but it is very special. Water is something we take for granted because it is so easy to come by. Sometimes we are that way by God. God is so easy to claim and receive that we take him for granted. After today, look at water in a different way. Love it, respect it, be thankful for it, and then remember to love God, and be thankful for him.

Prayer:

Now, bow your head, close your eyes, and let's talk to God. You say after me: **"Dear God, Thank you for water. Thank you for cleaning our hearts and souls. Amen."**

(I bought the 8 oz. bottles of water for the children. They are smaller and easier for them to handle than the larger sizes.)

#74
A Little Fish And A Little Faith
(Based on John 6:1-11)
(stewardship)

THEME: Give what you can, and let Jesus figure out what to do with it.

This is the time of year when we are encouraged to give to God and to give to others by giving to the church. You may wonder why that would have anything to do with you. Most of you probably don't have high paying jobs yet. How could you help support the church? Did you know that one of the most loved and talked about stories in the Bible is about a little boy around your age who gave enough to Jesus to feed over 5000 people? Let me tell you the story.

People followed Jesus around. They wanted to hear everything he had to say and watch everything he did because he was so special. Jesus needed some time by himself because someone he loved very much had just been killed, and he was sad. So, he got in a boat and crossed the Sea of Galilee to a place where he could be by himself for a little while. But before long, thousands of people had found him in the desert where he had gone. They had walked a long way, and there was no food around. Those thousands of people had gotten hungry.

Jesus put his sadness aside and tended to the people. He turned to his disciples and asked, "How are we going to feed these people out here in the desert?" even though he already knew. They talked about it and decided there was no way. They didn't have enough to even bother with. Andrew spoke up and said, "There's a little boy here who wants to give you his two little fish and five little loaves of bread, but what's that going to do? How is that going to feed over 5000 people?"

Now you know those disciples had more money, more strength, and way more experience than that little boy did, but they didn't have more faith. That little boy gave Jesus what he had and let Jesus figure out what to do with it. He didn't worry about how his little dinner could feed thousands of people. He just gave what he had. Jesus took those two little fish and those five little loves of bread and fed the entire crowd. The Bible says that everyone got full, and there were twelve baskets of leftovers. Jesus took a little dinner, given by a little boy, and performed a great big miracle with it.

That little boy probably didn't have any money, but he didn't let that stop him from giving Jesus what he had. He wasn't thinking about what his gift *couldn't* do, he was just thinking *what I can do.*

Bible Verse:

The Bible verse today comes from **John 6:11**. You say after me: **"Jesus took the loaves and the fish and gave thanks to God and passed them out to the people."**

A little boy gave what he had, and it made all the difference. What could you do? Share your time with a lonely person; bring someone to church with you. Share your lunch with someone who forgot their lunch money or left their lunch at home. You don't have a clue what Jesus could do with a kindness like that. You give what you can, and let Jesus figure out what to do with it.

Sermon Ending:

I brought each of you two fish cookies today. One is for you, and one is to share. Give it with love.

Devotional Ending:

Always remember to give with love in your heart and faith in Jesus.

Prayer:

Now, bow your head, close your eyes, and let's talk to God. You say after me: **"Dear God, Thank you for how you take our gifts and make them something special. Amen."**

(I traced a pattern of a whale from a coloring book to make a template for a cookie pattern. I frosted the sugar cookies with light blue icing.)

#75
Let's Talk About The Bible
Based on Psalms 119:105
(could be used the Sunday before Vacation Bible School begins — or anytime)

THEME: The Bible is about God's promises that have come to pass and those we can still look forward to.

(If you are not using this the Sunday before Vacation Bible School, omit the first sentence.) Vacation Bible School starts this week in our church, so I thought it would be a good idea to talk about the Bible today.

I thought you might want to know just what the Bible is. The Bible is a collection of books written by different people during a period of more than 1000 years. It is divided into two main parts: the Old Testament and the New Testament. The Old Testament books are the Scriptures of the Jewish people. They tell about the people of ancient Israel over hundreds of years. The New Testament is a collection of writings about Jesus and his first followers, and they cover a period of only about 60 or 70 years.

There are 66 books all together in the Bible. The Bible is sort of like a library in a way because it has so many kinds of writing in it. There are books about laws and history; there are poems and wise sayings. There are diaries and even letters.

The Old Testament has 39 books in it, and they are the Scriptures that Jesus read and studied. Christians read and study the Old Testament still today because of what we can learn about God, about others, and about ourselves. The Old Testament has a lot of promises in it from God, while the New Testament tells us how God made his promises come true.

Speaking of the New Testament, there are 27 books in it. The first four books are the gospels. The word GOSPEL means good news, and they are about the life and teachings of Jesus. There are books about the birth of the Christian church and the growth of the church, and how a church should behave. There are books about how to live for Christ Jesus, about faith, love, and the Holy Spirit. There are books about sin and the forgiveness of sin. The New Testament encourages us, it teaches us, and it has promises in it from God yet to come about.

Testament is a good name for the old part of the Bible and the new part, because the word TESTAMENT means promises, and the Bible is all about promises from God to us — some that have come to pass and some that we as Christians are still looking forward to.

The Bible is a library of books that are the key to life on earth and life after death. The Bible is sacred, the Bible is holy; the Bible is a gift from God. Study it, love it, live by it; keep it close to your heart.

Bible Verse:

The Bible verse today comes from **Psalms 119:105**. You say after me: "**Thy word is a lamp unto my feet and a light unto my path.**"

Sermon Ending:

I made each of you something for your Bible. It is a book

marker with our Bible verse on it today. I have book markers in my Bibles that friends have given me over the years, and they mark special places in the Bible that speak especially to me. I hope you will do that with this marker.

Devotional Ending:

Live by that verse. Let your Bible be a lamp unto your feet and a light unto your path. If you do, your future will be so much brighter.

Prayer:

Now, bow your head, close your eyes, and let's talk to God. You say after me: **"Dear God, Thank you for the Bible and for all it teaches us. Amen."**

(To make the markers, I simply took 4X6 lavender index cards and cut them in half — length wise. I printed the verse with a purple marker, glued a purple ribbon rose on one end, hole punched right above it and tied a purple ribbon through it. On the other end, I put an angel sticker. The ribbon roses come on a roll of ribbon that can be bought by the foot or roll in any fabric store or Walmart. I just snipped off the roses from the ribbon. Having the book markers laminated or covered in clear contact paper would make them more durable.)

#76
The Wind And The Spirit
Based on John 20:29
(could be used on a holiday where the flag is celebrated)

THEME: Things unseen can be very powerful, like the wind and the Holy Spirit.

I want to talk about something that is invisible — in other words, something you cannot see. This invisible thing can be strong or gentle, it can be cold or warm, and it can be nice or terrible. This invisible thing can pick up stuff and move it around. The thing I'm talking about can push over great big trees. It can even destroy whole cities! This thing can be pleasant or it can be frightening. This thing has a lot of power, and you never know when it is going to show up or from which direction it is coming. I am talking about the wind.

A lot of people don't want to believe in things they have never seen, but everyone believes in the wind, and you can't see it. You can see how the wind affects things and changes things. You can see the results of the wind, but you can't see the wind itself.

Now let me tell you about something else that is invisible, and it is even more powerful than the wind. I'm talking about the Holy Spirit. You can't see it, but it is all around you. The Holy Spirit is another name for God and Jesus.

Jesus lived on earth for awhile, but then he was killed — crucified. If you remember, however, he didn't stay dead. Jesus rose from the dead after three days, and he went to his disciples and said, "Go and make disciples in all the nations, baptizing them in the name of the Father, and of the Son, and of the Holy Spirit." He also said, "Be sure of this — that I am with you always even to the end of the world." Then he ascended into heaven to be with God.

When Jesus said he would be with us always, he meant he would be here in spirit. We aren't able to see him, but like the wind, he is with us — all around us. And do you know what makes the Holy Spirit more powerful than even the strongest wind? The Holy Spirit can change a person's heart; it can change a person's mind. It can change a person's life forever. Even though we can't see the Holy Spirit, we can see the results of it — how it affects and changes people.

Bible Verse:

The Bible verse today comes from **John 20:29**. You say after me: **"Blessed are those who haven't seen me and believe anyway."**

Believing in something you haven't seen is called faith. Have faith that the Holy Spirit is with you always. Let it live in you and around you. Let it guide you.

Sermon Ending:

On this Memorial Day (or July 4th) weekend, You might notice American flags blowing in the wind. I brought each of you a flag to help you remember that things unseen can be very powerful — like the wind and the Holy Spirit.

Devotional Ending:

When you see trees or flags or even feel your hair blowing in the wind, let it remind you that things unseen can be very powerful — like the wind and the Holy Spirit.

Prayer:

Now, bow your head, close your eyes, and let's talk to God. You say after me: **"Dear God, Help me to feel your Holy Spirit in my life. Amen."**

(Walmart usually has packets of the small American flags, or you can find them in the Oriental Trading Catalog. *If you live in another country, you could use this lesson on a holiday where you display the flag of your country to celebrate, or you could just omit the holiday part and talk about flags blowing, etc.)*

#77

Heart Full Of Love
Based on Luke 6:45
(for the Sunday before Valentine's Day)

THEME: Let God determine your destiny.

One of my most favorite days is February 14th. Does anyone know what day that is? Valentine's Day! That's right. I like Valentine's Day because it focuses on the heart. You see, the heart is where people store their love, and Valentine's Day is about loving others. Special days, like Valentine's Day, help call our attention to things we sometimes overlook, like *showing* someone we love them and appreciate them.

Have you ever wondered why God chose to store our love in our heart? I think maybe he did it because the heart is the organ in our body that keeps us alive. If our heart quit beating, we would die. And you know what, love is as important as heartbeats. Everyone wants love, and everyone needs love.

I want to teach you a new word today. The word is DESTINY. Say it for me: DESTINY. The dictionary defines destiny as a predetermined course of events. In other words — after all is said and done — it's where you end up and how you lived your life to get there.

If you hope that your destiny is to end up in heaven with God someday, let God direct your actions. Let God fill your heart to the brim with love.

Bible Verse:

The Bible verse today comes from **Luke 6:45.** You say after me: "**A good man produces good deeds from a good heart. Whatever is in the heart overflows into speech.**"

Did you know that * *A loving heart affects your thoughts. Your thoughts become words. Watch you words — they turn into actions, and your actions become habits. Your habits — well your habits mold your character, and your character determines your destiny.*

Sermon Ending:

I made each of you some heart-shaped cookies to remind you how sweet life is if you let God fill your heart with love.

Devotional Ending:

Let God determine your destiny by asking Jesus to live in your heart.

Prayer:

Now, bow your head, close your eyes, and let's talk to God. You say after me: "**Dear God, Fill my heart with love. Control my destiny with your love. Amen.**"

(Pink icing on your cookies will make them look and taste especially good. Also, most grocery stores and bakeries have Valentine cookies already made if you had rather buy them.)

(*Paraphrased from a quote written by Frank Outlaw.)

#78

Lend A Helping Hand
Based on I Timothy 5:4
(Halloween theme)

THEME: Lend a helping hand, and you will receive the blessing.

(Presenter might take a carved and lighted pumpkin for display. There are many stencil designs now that don't promote grim ideas, if that is a concern.) There is a holiday coming up this week. What is it? It is Halloween. It's a holiday where people dress up in costumes, carve pumpkins, and go trick-or-treating. Those are all fun things to do, but I would like for you to add something else to your list of fun things to do on Halloween. I want you to lend a helping hand to others on Halloween.

It is actually fun to help others if you do it for the right reasons. If you help someone because somebody makes you do it, well, that probably wouldn't be very enjoyable. But if you decide in your heart that you want to help that person, it turns out to be a blessing for you.

What are some ways that you could help someone? *(Let chil-*

dren *answer then add the ones listed that they didn't mention.)* You could put things back where they belong, straighten up your room or another room at the end of the day, help carry in the groceries, and feed and water pets. When one of your parents tells you to do something, do it with a smile, and don't argue. Another helpful thing to do is not fight with your brother or sister because it disturbs the peace in the house.

Bible Verse:

The Bible verse today comes from **I Timothy 5:4**. You say after me: "**. . . kindness should begin at home helping parents. This pleases God very much.**"

Sermon Ending:

To remind you to lend a helping hand, I made each of you a Halloween hand.

Devotional Ending:

Lend a helping hand this Halloween and every day after that. You will be the one that receives the greatest blessing.

Prayer:

Now, bow your head, close your eyes, and let's talk to God. You say after me: "**Dear God, Keep me faithful. Help me to help others. Amen.**"

(Make Halloween hands using clear disposable gloves like the ones used for dyeing hair or handling food. Check grocery stores or beauty supply stores. Drop a piece of candy corn in each finger for the fingernails, then stuff the whole thing with popcorn. Use black and orange ribbon to tie up the end and include a Halloween lollipop. Decorate one of the fingers with a spider ring. The flavored popcorn that comes in decorative cans works well and offers a variety of colors. You can use the can to transport the hands. The Oriental Trading Catalog *has spider rings.)*

#79
The Greatest Gift Of All
Based on I Corinthians 13:8
(Mother's Day)

THEME: Give your mother your love. It is the greatest gift of all.

Today is a special day. It is Mother's Day. It is the day we celebrate our love for our mothers and our mother's love for us.

Mothers love their children in many different ways. You know, love is not just a warm fuzzy feeling. Love is action. Love is taking care of you when you are hurt or sick. Love is making sure you are where you need to be. Love is running errands for the family like grocery shopping after working all day. Love is keeping your clothes washed and making sure you have shoes to wear. Love is teaching you right from wrong, and sometimes love is about fussing at you when you do wrong or hugging you when you do something just right. Love is about making sure you get fed, and sometimes a mother's love comes in the form of an ice cream cone.

Love is doing; love is giving. Sometimes a mother's love is

tough, and sometimes a mother's love is soft and cuddly. But a mother's love is always a precious thing. So, if you have a mother, take the time to thank her today for all the ways she shows her love for you.

Bible Verse:

The Bible verse today comes from **I Corinthians 13:8**. You say after me: **"All the special gifts and powers from God will someday come to an end, but love goes on forever."**

It would be nice if you could give your mother a beautiful and expensive present on Mother's Day, but do you know what mothers want more than anything else? Your love.

Sermon Ending:

Give your mother this little heart today, and tell her that you love her with all your heart. You see, love is the greatest gift of all.

Devotional Ending:

Tell your mother that you love her, then show her by being obedient and respectful. And even when you can give your mother a beautiful and expensive present, never forget that love is the greatest gift of all.

Prayer:

Now, bow your head, close your eyes, and let's talk to God. You say after me: **"Dear God, Thank you for mothers. Thank you for all the ways they show their love. Amen."**

(I found some little red hearts, 12 or 14 to a package, but you could cut out felt hearts, make heart-shaped cookies, or even have a red carnation for each child to give their mother.)

#80
Operating Instructions
Based on Exodus 20:12
(for Mother's Day)

THEME: Honor your mother.
    Listen to this story about a lady whose oven went out. She had to buy a new one, and the one she bought had a smooth top and two separate ovens. The panel across the back had this key pad where she had to touch certain buttons to program it — make it do what she wanted it to, when she wanted it to — and quite frankly, it was complicated. Luckily for her, it came with operating instructions.
    Most things do come with operating instructions, especially if they are complicated pieces of equipment, and if you follow the instructions, they usually work and act the way you expect them to. However, the most complicated new thing the lady in the story ever brought home came with absolutely no operating instructions. It had all kinds of mechanisms that when activated made all sorts of noises and stuff. And these mechanisms were

self-starting and nonprogramable. It was her baby. Several years ago, she went to the hospital, gave birth to a baby boy, brought him home, and didn't have a clue what to do with him. He did not have a control panel with buttons to push that would make him act or do what she wanted him to.

As a baby grows into a big boy or girl your size, they get even more complicated. You have likes and dislikes; you have to be taught right from wrong, and sometimes you need repairs. If only you came with operating instructions!

Bible Verse:

The Bible verse today comes from **Exodus 20:12**. You say after me: "**Honor your father and mother.**"

Today, Mother's Day, is a day to honor mothers — not because moms are perfect or because we/they always know how to operate or handle our/their children. It is because we/they don't. Mothers make mistakes. Mothers don't know all the answers. Mothers lose their tempers. Mothers forget things. Mothers burn dinner sometimes even in brand-new ovens — especially in brand-new ovens.

Honor your mother — not because she does everything right, but because she gets up everyday and tries to do everything right — even without instructions.

Sermon Ending:

I brought each of you a chocolate *ladybug* today to remind you to honor your mother, even when the *lady bugs* you.

Devotional Ending:

It is what God wants you to do.

Prayer:

Now, bow your head, close your eyes, and let's talk to God. You say after me: "**Dear God, Thank you for mothers. Amen.**"

(LOOK FOR THE LADYBUGS! I found them in packages at The World Market. I have seen candy stores in malls that carry candy like this and others I have mentioned. If you can't find candy lady-

bugs, you could easily make some ladybugs out of red and black construction paper or find some ladybug stickers or erasers. The Oriental Trading Catalog *has several ladybug items.)*

#81
Taping What Is Torn
Based on Luke 15
(Father's Day — the prodigal son story from the father's point of view)

THEME: God can tape your life back together when it has been torn all apart.

Since today is Father's Day, I thought I would tell you a Bible story about a good father. This particular father had a lot of money, a lot of land, and a lot of people who worked for him, but what he was most proud of were his two sons. He had planned for each of them to get half of all he owned someday. He didn't want them to ever have to worry about having a home or enough money. As they got older, he taught them the family business and let them work for him.

One of his sons enjoyed working with his dad, but the other son grew tired of it quickly. He wanted to party and travel and spend money on girls who didn't act very nice. He told his father that he wanted his money right then, and he would be out of there.

This father knew his son would probably waste all that money and get into trouble of one kind or another, and sure enough, that is what happened. It wasn't long before that young man had spent every last cent of his money. He wound up a long way from home working on a pig farm feeding nasty pigs. He had gotten so poor and hungry that he caught himself wanting to eat the yucky pig feed he was feeding the pigs. He was scared, he was lonely, and he was ashamed of the bad choices he had made. He decided to go home and beg his daddy to just let him work for him as one of the hired hands, and he wouldn't expect him to treat him like his son again because he had wasted all his money and done some terribly ugly things while he had been away.

So he started the long journey home, and when he finally got to the far end of his father's property, his father recognized him in the distance. Love and pure joy flooded that father's heart when he saw his son. He ran as fast as he could to his child who had been lost and torn apart his life. With love and forgiveness, he wrapped his arms around his child and said, "Son, welcome home!"

Not everyone has a father like that at home. Not everyone is capable of that kind of love and forgiveness, but Jesus told that story to teach us that we all have a father like that in heaven, and his name is God.

Bible Verse:

The Bible verse today comes from **Luke 15:21**. You say after me: **"I am not worthy to be called your son."**

No one behaves good enough to deserve the kind of love God has for us. You see, God is love!

Sermon Ending:

I brought each of you a roll of tape today. Like tape, forgiveness and love can put things back together that have been torn apart. Let this tape remind you that God can tape your life back

together when you tear it all apart.
Devotional Ending:
No one behaves good enough to deserve the kind of love God has for us. You see, God is love! *(Presenter should hold up a plastic dispenser of tape here.)* Like tape, forgiveness and love can put things back together that have been torn apart. God can tape your life back together when you tear it all apart.
Prayer:
Now, bow your head, close your eyes, and let's talk to God. You say after me: **"Dear God, Thank you for the way your love and forgiveness holds me together. Amen."**

(I found four rolls of tape in dispensers in a package at Dollar Tree. The Oriental Trading Catalog *also has rolls of tape.)*

#82
Make A Joyful Noise
Based on Psalms 100:1-2
(for the Sunday the church choir sings their special Christmas music)

THEME: Music can polish your soul.

(If your church does not participate in Advent rituals, just omit the sentences about Advent and replace them with Christmas season.) This is the second Sunday of Advent. The Advent Season is the celebration of the coming of Jesus to this world as a human being. There are many ways that we can celebrate. We can go to Christmas parties, we can give gifts to people in celebration of the birthday of Christ Jesus. Stores, businesses, churches, and our homes are decorated with lights and flowers and Christmas trees as part of the celebration.

Another very special way we celebrate the coming of Jesus is through singing. Music. . . Let's think about music. Music comes in many forms. There are all kinds of musical instruments that have different sounds, and there is a wide variety of different styles of music. However, I don't think there is a more beautiful sound in the world than the sound of sweet voices singing praises to God.

Music is a gift to us from God. God blesses each of us with different gifts. Some people he blessed with a special talent for playing musical instruments or singing. Even if you can't carry a tune in a bucket, you can listen to music. By listening to music, we can become part of its beauty and inspiration. Music can reach inside you and polish your soul. God gave us music to enjoy, and when we give it back to him in the form of praise, it shows God that we love him and appreciate his greatness.

Bible Verse:

The Bible verse today comes from **Psalms 100:1-2**. You say after me: **"Make a joyful noise unto the Lord, serve the Lord with gladness: come before his presence with singing."**

In our church we have several choirs: the bell choir, the children's choirs, which many of you are a part of, and the church choir. Today our church choir is going to exalt God. To exalt God means they are going to glorify, praise, and honor God, and they are going to do it by singing special Christmas music. By our being here to listen, we can feel closer to Jesus and be inspired to try harder to be good and loving Christians.

For those of you who stay in the sanctuary today, listen to the choir's music with your ears, but also with your heart, because it can lift you up, polish your soul, and bring you closer to Jesus. Christmas music — what a wonderful way to celebrate the advent season!

Sermon Ending:

I brought each of you a little whistle today so that you can make a joyful noise unto the Lord. This little whistle is made out of candy. I hope it will remind you that there is nothing sweeter than music to God's ears. *(As the whistles are being passed out, presenter could play "Joy to the World" on the candy whistle. It will take a little practice, but it is not difficult — even if you can't carry a tune*

in a bucket.)
Devotional Ending:
What a wonderful way to remind us that there is nothing sweeter than music to God's ears.
Prayer:
Now, bow your head, close your eyes, and let's talk to God. You say after me: "**Dear God, Fill my heart with music, and polish my soul with its beauty. Amen.**"

(The whistles are called "Melody Pops" and they are made by Chupa Chups. I found them at Dollar Tree, but many convenience stores and even restaurants sell Chupa Chups lollipops and would probably get you a box of the Melody Pops, with enough notice, from their candy supplier. They are fun and easy to play even if you aren't musically inclined. If you can't find the Melody Pops, the Oriental Trade Catalog *has plastic slide flutes sold by the dozen.)*

#83
Rejoice, Rejoice
Based on Matthew 1:21

THEME: Lead a life that lends beauty and grace to Jesus.
(This could be used for the 3rd Sunday of Advent.) I read a story the other day that I'd like to tell you about. I want to tell you this story today because this is the third Sunday of advent — focusing on and feeling the joy of the coming of Christmas — rejoicing in the birth of Jesus. You see, this story is about Jesus, and it went something like this: *(Based on the anonymous essay, "One Solitary Life." I have paraphrased it for children.)*

Jesus was born in a little village, the child of a poor, young, unmarried peasant woman. He grew up and worked in a carpenter shop until he was thirty years old, and then for three years he was a walk-around-preacher. He never wrote a book. He never held an office. He never owned a home. He never had a wife or children. He never went to college. He never traveled more than 200 miles from the place he was born. He didn't have the things or do the things we usually associate with a person of importance or greatness.

While he was still a young man, the people turned against him. His friends ran away. He was handed over to his enemies and went through a trial that wasn't fair. He was nailed to a cross between two common thieves. While he was dying on that cross, the people who nailed him up there gambled for the only piece of property he had on earth, and that was his coat. When he was dead, he was laid in a borrowed grave.

Two thousand years have come and gone since then, and today Jesus is still the most celebrated, honored, important, and talked about person that ever walked on this earth. Out of all the armies that ever marched into battle, all the navies that ever sailed the seas, all the kings or presidents that ever ruled, all together they have not affected the life of people on this earth as that one little baby who grew up to be the Savior of the world.

Anonymous
(paraphrased)

That is where the rejoicing comes in. God sent us our Savior in the form of a little baby who grew up to be the most powerful life in the world. He didn't do it with money or armies or violence or false promises. He did it with love and patience; with hope and forgiveness. He did it with God.

Bible Verse:

The Bible verse today comes from **Matthew 1:21.** You say after me: **"Mary will have a son, and you shall name him Jesus, meaning savior, for he will save his people from their sins."**

Be one of **his** people.

Sermon Ending:

Do you know what an ornament is? It is something that

lends grace or beauty to something else, like a tree ornament makes the Christmas tree more beautiful. I brought each of you a chocolate Christmas tree ornament. Let it remind you to live a life that lends grace and beauty and sweetness to Jesus.

Devotional Ending:

Do you know what an ornament is? It is something that lends grace or beauty to something else, like a tree ornament makes the Christmas tree more beautiful. When you look at your Christmas tree this year, let it remind you to live a life that lends grace and beauty to Jesus.

Prayer:

Now, bow your head, close your eyes, and let's talk to God. You say after me: **"Dear God, We rejoice in your son, Jesus. Help us to be ornaments of grace and beauty for him. Amen."**

(Any Christmas tree ornament would do fine. I had found some chocolate ornaments at The World Market, so I gave the children those. Real ones would probably be even better.)

#84

Legend Of The Poinsettia
Based on Song of Solomon 8:7
(to be used one or two Sundays before Christmas)

THEME: God can turn your love into something beautiful.

(Presenter will need to have a red poinsettia for the children to see.) I want to tell you a story about a little girl named Christina. She lived in a small village in Mexico with her mother, and they were very poor. Christina didn't have nice dresses to wear. In fact, they were torn and tattered and threadbare. She had no shoes at all, but what she did have was a loving heart.

When Christina turned six years old, her mother started letting her walk to church by herself. Her mother was sick and unable to go, but she had taught Christina to love God. Christmas time came, and all the people in the church were to bring gifts on Christmas Eve night in honor of the Christ Child, the baby Jesus.

The altar had been decorated with a nativity scene, and Christina could hardly wait for Christmas Eve. She went home and told her mother all about it. With tears in her eyes, her mother had to tell Christina that she had no money to buy any Christmas gifts at all. Christina was disappointed, but she understood.

Christmas Eve finally came, and Christina started out for her walk to the church. She wanted more than anything to have an offering to take, but she had nothing. On her journey she noticed some green weeds growing alongside the road, and her heart filled with joy. She began to pick those weeds until she had all that her little hands would hold. Barefooted, she entered the church to offer her gift for the Christ Child.

As Christina got closer to the altar, she saw that it was filled with beautiful and expensive gifts, and tears began to fall from her eyes. She realized that her gift was worthless. Embarrassed and ashamed, Christina turned to leave. But a member of the church reached out to the barefooted little girl and led her to the altar where she innocently laid her bundle of weeds.

The service began. The minister spoke, the choir sang, and then they all bowed to pray. After the prayer the people opened their eyes and to their amazement, on the altar, the weeds Christina had brought had turned crimson red. The people were amazed at what had happened.

You see, God had taken the innocent love-gift from a little child and turned it into something beautiful, and legend has it that every year at Christmas time these plants turn bright red because a little girl had pure love in her heart for Jesus.

I don't know if the story about Christina is true or not, but I do know that if you love God, he always turns your love into something beautiful.

Bible Verse:

The Bible verse today comes from **Song of Solomon 8:7**. You say after me: "**If a man tried to buy love with everything he owned, he couldn't do it.**"

Sermon Ending:

I brought each of you some play money today. You can't buy anything with it, but it's to remind you that money can't buy love. Love must come from your heart, and God will take that love and turn it into something beautiful.

Devotional Ending:

Money can't buy love. Love must come from the heart, and God will take that love and turn it into something beautiful.

Prayer:

Now, bow your head, close your eyes, and let's talk to God. You say after me: "**Dear God, Help me to value love over money. Turn my love into something beautiful. Amen.**"

(Use play paper money. Roll it and tie it with red and/or green ribbon and attach a small Christmas ornament, like a white dove.)

#85
Legend Of The Candy Cane
Based on Luke 2:1-11
(to be used one or two Sundays before Christmas)

THEME: Keep "Christ" in Christmas.

Have you ever wondered why candy canes are so popular at Christmas time? Well, there is a reason for it. You see, there was a candymaker in the state of Indiana who wanted to make a candy that was special for Christmas. He wanted it to remind people that Christmas is about Jesus, so he decided to make his candy in the shape of the letter "J." *(Presenter should hold up a large candy cane as a prop from here on so children can visually see what is being described.)* You know, that is the first letter in the name Jesus.

If you turn the "J" upside down, it looks like the curved staff or cane that shepherds used to tend their flocks of sheep. Did you know that God sent an angel to tell some certain shepherds first about the birth of Jesus? The angel said, "For unto you is born this day in the city of David, a Savior, which is Christ the Lord." *(Presenter will show a picture of shepherds with canes. These are easily found on Christmas cards.)*

The candymaker made the "J" white to symbolize the purity and goodness of Jesus.

When the angel told that the Savior was born, the angel knew that Jesus would grow up to die on the cross for all our sins. When the time came for Jesus to do that, he was whipped across his back and chest, leaving bloody stripes around his body. So the candymaker put three small stripes on his candy cane to remind us of the pain Jesus suffered for us.

The bold red stripe symbolizes the blood Jesus shed for us while nailed to the cross.

Today, a lot of people don't know why we buy candy canes at Christmas time or why we hang them on our Christmas trees, but it was because a candymaker wanted us to remember that Christmas is the celebration of the birth of Christ Jesus, God's gift to us.

Bible Verse:

The Bible verse today comes from **Luke 2:11**. You say after me: **"For unto you is born this day in the city of David, a Savior, which is Christ the Lord."** And that, my little friends, is what Christmas is all about.

Sermon Ending:

I brought each of you a candy cane to hang on your Christmas tree to remind you that Christmas is about Christ Jesus.

Devotional Ending:

If you get a candy cane for Christmas, share the legend of the candy cane with the person who gives it you. Let them know it is about Jesus.

Prayer:

Now, bow you head, close your eyes, and let's talk to God. You say after me: **"Dear God, Thank you for the birth of Jesus. Help us to keep Christ in Christmas. Amen."**

(Try to find large and substantial candy canes that will not break easily. Also, they must be in the shape of a cane and not just a stick. I have only found them separately and not in value boxes.)

#86
The Light Of The World
Based on Luke 2:1-20 and John 12:46
(Christmas Eve)

THEME: Jesus came to this world to be our light in the darkness.

Today is a holy day. It is Christmas Eve, and our fourth Advent candle has been lit. Its light represents Jesus' promise of salvation — in other words, his promise to bring us to heaven when we die. Its light. . .

We are going to talk about light today. When God decided to create the heavens and earth, the first thing he did was say, "Let there be light," and light appeared. The Bible says God was pleased with it and divided the light from the darkness.

When God wanted to announce the birth of Jesus, the Bible says that God sent an angel to some shepherds who were tending their sheep at night and the angel appeared in a light so bright that it lit up the darkness. Then the sky filled up with lots and lots of angels, and they sang praises to God, and light shone all around them. Light . . .

Light has other meanings too. Light means understanding. Light represents what is good, pure, true, and holy. On the other hand, darkness represents sin and evil.

God is so organized, and it was no mistake or accident that his son, the Messiah, the Savior, the King of Kings, was born in a dark and dirty stable. God planned it that way. You see, Jesus, the baby king was pure and true and holy. He was light — the light of the world. By being born in a dark, dirty stable, it shows us that Jesus came to this world to be our light in the darkness — to make what is dirty and ugly in our lives clean, and it matters not who we are or where we live.

Bible Verse:

The Bible verse today comes from **John 12:46**. You say after me: **"I have come as a light to shine in this dark world, so that all who put their trust in me will no longer wander in the darkness."**

As Christians we are to be light bearers, letting the light of Jesus shine through us. It doesn't matter who we are or where we live or how much money we have or don't have. The very first people God chose to tell about the birth of his son, Jesus, were some poor humble shepherds who lived outside with their sheep — plain ordinary people just doing their job, tending their little lambs, and an angel of God appeared in the sky to tell them the news that the Lamb of God, the Messiah, the Savior, the Light of the World had been born. And we call that Christmas.

Sermon Ending:

(You will need to adjust the following to fit your situation and your gift. See my notes at the bottom.) My husband and I made you something that we hope will help you remember that Jesus is your light in the darkness. It is a stained-glass night light. It represents the angel of the Lord that announced the birth of Jesus, the Light of the World.

Devotional Ending:

Let Jesus be your light in the darkness.

Prayer:

Now, bow your head, close your eyes, and let's talk to God. You say after me: **"Dear God, Let the light of Jesus shine through me. Thank you for Christmas. Amen."**

Merry Christmas! Go forth and let your little light shine.

(Stained glass is a hobby for my husband and me. We wanted to make something special for the children. There are any number of things you could make or buy that would represent light for this lesson. A little candle would be an excellent idea or even a candle made out of felt.)

#87
An Eye On God
Based on Psalms 57:7-11
(for the Sunday before New Year's Day)

THEME: Keep an eye on God, and he will keep an eye on you.

(Tomorrow) is the first day of a brand new year. It is going to be the first day of the year (----). You may hear people talk about New Year's Resolutions. Let me tell you what that means when they say that. To make a New Year's Resolution is to make a promise to yourself to do something important that has been hard for you to do before. For example: some people make themselves a promise to lose weight or stop smoking, or it could be to visit a sick person once a week or to not talk ugly to or about others. Whatever the promise, it is usually made to yourself, and it should be a good thing to do. The hard part is keeping the promise.

People like new beginnings and new years because it gives us the feeling that we can erase the past and have a new start at trying to do things right that we have not been good at before.

However, I have discovered something about promises I make to myself or others. If I leave God out of it, the promise is much harder to keep. If I promise God that I am going to do or not do something, it becomes much more serious than if I just promise myself.

God wants us to respect him like we respect our parents. When I was little, I knew there were things I had better not do or my mother would have spanked me. I had a fear of that so it made me act better and keep my promises to her. I knew when she said, "Don't play with matches," she meant it, and I would have been in trouble if I had. The deal is, she always had my safety and well-being in mind, and that is the way God is. God wants us to do the right thing and keep our promises for our own good and the good of others.

Bible Verse:

The Bible verse today comes from **Psalms 57:10**. You say after me: **"God's kindness and love are as big as the heavens. His faithfulness is higher than the skies."**

It is a good idea to try and be a better person every new year, but if you are serious about it, make God part of it. Make your promises to God and not just to yourself. Always keep an eye on God, and he will keep an eye on you and help you in any situation. Choose to be a child of God's.

Sermon Ending:

I brought you something for this new year to help you remember to include God in your promises, in your behavior, in your life. It is an eye that you can stick on a mirror or a window in your room. Remember to keep an eye on God all the time, and he will keep an eye on you.

Devotional Ending:

Choose to be a better person this new year with God's help.

Prayer:

Now, bow your head, close your eyes, and let's talk to God.

How To Talk To Children About God

You say after me: "**Dear God, Help me to be good this year. Keep a watchful eye on me. Amen.**"

(I gave each child a plastic eye with a suction cup on the back They came from the Oriental Trading Catalog.*)*

#88

Gold, Frankincense, And Myrrh
Based on Matthew 2:11
(to be used for Epiphany or at Christmas time, if your church does not observe Epiphany)

THEME: Find ways to honor Jesus.

We have talked about an angel from God announcing the birth of Jesus to some shepherds who were tending their sheep, and how they went to visit and worship the baby Jesus. Well, the shepherds weren't the only visitors the baby Jesus had. There were three kings who traveled a long way, following a star to find the Christ Child. These three kings were called the Three Wise Men because they were very smart. *(Presenter should show a picture of the Three Wise Men riding camels. This is a common scene on Christmas cards.)* These three kings, the Wise Men, have also been called Magi which means they studied the stars. When the three Wise Men found the baby Jesus, the Bible tells us that each one gave him a present. One of the kings gave him gold, another one gave him frankincense, and the third Wise Man gave him myrrh.

You probably know what gold is, but do you know what frankincense and myrrh are? I assumed you might not, so I brought some to show you.

Frankincense comes from a small tree. People slash the roots and branches, and gum oozes out, hardening in lumps like this. It was burned in the form of incense in religious ceremonies, and it was also made into medicines and perfumes. *(Pass around the frankincense for children to touch and smell while you are talking about it. See my notes at the bottom on where to find frankincense and myrrh.)*

Myrrh is also a resin, but it comes from a bush. *(Now pass around the myrrh.)* It was used much the same way as frankincense, and both were expensive and treasured items.

This is gold. *(Pass gold coins, like the Sacagawea coins or gold foil-wrapped candy coins, around in a little treasure chest or jewelry type chest.)* Gold, of course, could be used for money or jewelry and was a very fitting gift for a king. Frankincense was considered to be a gift for a deity, a God, and myrrh was a gift for one who was to die. All three gifts were appropriate because Jesus was a king, he was a deity, and since he was born to be our Savior, he would die for our sins.

Bible Verse:

The Bible verse today comes from **Matthew 2:11**. You say after me: "**The three Wise Men opened their presents and gave baby Jesus gold, frankincense, and myrrh.**"

Sermon Ending:

To help you remember the Magi, who we also call the Three Kings or the Three Wise Men, I brought you some (candy or plastic) gold coins.

Devotional Ending:

As you grow physically and spiritually, be mindful of gifts you can give to Jesus by giving to others.

Prayer:

Goldfish and Silver Kisses

Now, bow your head, close your eyes, and let's talk to God. You say after me: **"Dear God, Help me to find ways to honor Jesus. Amen."**

*(Frankincense and myrrh can be ordered from **Pacific Spirit's** catalog by calling 1-800-634-9057 or ordered from **Art & Culture, P.O. Box: 476, Dubai — U.A.E.** or by calling **971-4-219 339**, or **Fax 971-4 -272 318**.) It can be purchased in a beautiful wooden chest for approximately $35:00 to $45:00, or you can just purchase the refill for about $20:00. You can use this year after year, and it makes such an impression on the children. Many adults will have never seen it either. Both come in the same chest, so I separated them and put one in a different, yet beautiful, container. As an option, find out if anyone in your church has been to the Holy Land. The chest of frankincense and myrrh is a common souvenir item bought there. They might let you use theirs.)*

(The gold Sacagawea dollars, that you can get at any bank, work great for the gold coins. A bank will order rolls of new coins with enough prior notice, and they will be bright and shiny. I used chocolate coins wrapped in gold foil to look like real gold coins. I put 8 candy coins in little snack-size zip-lock bags. If you give them the candy coins, tell them to remove the foil before they eat them. You can also order plastic gold coins out of the Oriental Trading Catalog. *You may prefer to give each child one of the gold Sacagawea coins instead.)*

#89
Who Were Those Guys?
Based on Matthew 2:1-12
(Epiphany or Christmas time)

THEME: The Three Kings were wise; they came to worship Jesus.

Today in our church, we are celebrating Epiphany — the coming of the Magi, the Wise Men, to worship the Christ Child. While preparing for this lesson, I tried to find out just who those wise men were, and where exactly they came from. I mean, a big deal has been made of those guys year after year, and I wanted to know something about them. Well, I looked and I read and I researched, and the truth is, I don't know much more about who they were and exactly where they came from than I did before I started. That made me realize something. When Matthew wrote about the Magi, the wise men, he simply said they came from far away eastern lands, following a special star, and that they had come to worship the Christ Child, bringing gifts of gold, frankincense, and myrrh to honor him. Perhaps Matthew didn't tell us more about the Magi because that is not who or what we should focus on. Perhaps he wanted us to remember the important part only — that they were wise, and they had come to worship the baby Jesus.

Perhaps Matthew told us what the gifts were that the Magi brought because gold, frankincense, and myrrh were most valuable items in those times — precious and significant gifts — and it was his way of teaching us to give to Jesus the best that we have to offer.

Bible Verse:

The Bible verse today comes from **Matthew 2:11**. You say after me: **"They bowed down and worshiped him. Then they opened their gifts and gave him gold, frankincense, and myrrh."**

Let the story of the Wise Men be a lesson to you that God reaches people near and far, and that while we are asking for his blessings, his help, love, guidance, patience, and forgiveness, let us remember to sometimes just come to him with a gift, come to him with an offering, rather than always asking for something. The Magi were called wise men for a reason.

I want to pass around some frankincense and myrrh for you to see and smell. They are resins that were used as medicines, in cosmetics, perfumes, and in preparing the dead to be buried. They were worth their weight in gold. *(See my notes at the bottom on where to find frankincense and myrrh.)*

Sermon Ending:

I brought each of you a gold coin today that is worth a dollar. It represents the other gift of the Magi. You may want to keep your coin as a reminder to sometimes give to Jesus instead of always just asking for something, or sometime you may want to put your coin in the offering plate and practice giving to Jesus like once some very wise men did long, long ago.

Devotional Ending:

(If you are doing this ending, you will want to show the children

an example of gold along with the frankincense and myrrh.) Practice giving to Jesus like once some very wise men did long, long ago.
Prayer:

Now, bow your head, close your eyes, and let's talk to God. You say after me: **"Dear God, Let the lessons of the Magi teach us to honor Jesus with our worship and with our gifts. Amen."**

(The coins I mentioned were the Sacagawea gold dollars. With notice, the bank can get you some new ones so they will be bright and shiny. Frankincense and myrrh can be ordered from **Pacific Spirit's** *catalog by calling* **1-800-634-9057** *or ordered from* **Art & Culture, P.O. Box: 476, Dubai — U.A.E.** *or by calling 971-4-219 339, or* **Fax 9714 -272 318.***) It can be purchased in a beautiful wooden chest for approximately $35:00 to $45:00, or you can just purchase the refill for about $20:00. You can use this year after year, and it makes such an impression on the children. Many adults will have never seen it either. Both come in the same chest, so I separated them and put one in a different, yet beautiful, container. As an option, find out if anyone in your church has been to the Holy Land. The chest of frankincense and myrrh is a common souvenir item bought there. They might let you use theirs.)*

#90
Make It A Holy Week
Based on I Peter 1:15
(the week beginning on Palm Sunday and ending on Easter)

THEME: Christians need to be mindful of the events that led to the cross.

I want to show you something that is holy. This is my son's favorite pair of shorts. *(The presenter, of course, will need to alter the story according to whose shorts or shirt, etc., they use.)* The last time he came home from college, I washed his clothes for him. Do you want to know what else I did? I left these out of his laundry basket on purpose because they have so many holes in them. I didn't want Luke walking around in public in holy britches.

I brought these to show you what the word holy can mean. But there is another meaning for the word holy. Holy can also mean sacred and worthy of someone's absolute love and respect. It means Godly, and this is the definition of the word holy that I want to talk to you about today. You see, today is the first day of Holy Week. We call today Palm Sunday because it celebrates the story of Jesus riding into Jerusalem on a donkey and people spreading palm branches and clothes on the road in front of him as he rode into the holy city.

This coming Thursday is called Maundy Thursday and recalls the Last Supper of Jesus with his disciples where he gave them bread and wine to represent his body and his blood.

The next day, Friday, is Good Friday. It is the day Jesus was crucified, nailed to the cross, and died for our sins.

The following day is Holy Saturday when Christians remember the burial of Jesus, and then comes Easter Sunday when Jesus rose from the dead to be our Lord and Savior.

Holy Week is a week where Christians need to be especially mindful of the events that led up to the most amazing thing Jesus ever did for us — when he died on the cross so that we as Christians could go to heaven to live again after our time on earth is over.

Bible Verse:

The Bible verse today comes from **I Peter 1:15**. You say after me: **"Be holy now in everything you do, just as the Lord is holy."**

Sermon Ending:

I brought each of you a cross today. On each cross it says: *Jesus Christ is Lord.* I want you to carry it in your pocket or purse or backpack every day of this Holy Week to remind you that Jesus died on the cross for you and for me, but now he lives again. A little card goes with your cross, and I want to read the poem that is on it. *(Presenter will read the poem, "I Carry A Cross In My Pocket." It is printed on the card that comes with the cross, available at Christian book stores that carry Swanson materials. The card number is listed below. If you cannot find these, adjust ending accordingly. I cannot print the poem due to copyright laws.)*

Devotional Ending:

I bought this cross at a Christian book store to carry in my purse or pocket. I'd like to share with you the poem that came with it, and perhaps it will inspire you to carry a cross in your pocket.

(See explanation above.)
Prayer:
Now, bow your head, close your eyes, and let's talk to God. You say after me: **"Dear God, Thank you for Jesus. Help me to keep this week holy for him. Amen."**

(I found the crosses and cards at a Christian book store. They are sold together. The card with the poem is Swanson # 37133-1257.)

#91
It's All In God's Hands
Based on Mark 11:1-11
(Palm Sunday)

THEME: Sometimes our greatest gifts from God are when he says, "No."

Have you ever heard the song He's got the whole world in his hands, He's got the whole wide world in his hands? *(Presenter should sing those two lines.)* Who do you think He is in that song? It's God. God has the whole world in his hands. That's how big God is! *(Presenter should have a small globe in the palm of his hand. A variety of different little globes are available through the* Oriental Trading Catalog.*)*

That song goes on to say he's got you and me in his hands. It means that God is there for us and will take care of us if we will let him.

Whenever we pray for things, sometimes God says yes to our prayers, and sometimes he says no. Have you ever wondered why that is? It's because God sees the whole picture. He knows what lies ahead, and he knows what is best for us when often times we

Goldfish and Silver Kisses

don't. People sometimes choose only to see what is right in front of them and want what will make their life better and easier for the moment without considering their future or the future of others.

On this Palm Sunday, I'm reminded of Jesus' trip to Jerusalem on the back of a little donkey. Jerusalem was filled with Jews from all over the Roman Empire for the Passover celebration, and they had heard that this man, Jesus, was coming. Most of them believed that Jesus was the king God had promised he would send them.

When he arrived, those people were so excited that they threw down coats and palm branches on the road for him to ride across, showing that they honored him. But then — **there was a problem**. They thought God had sent them a king to deliver them from the problems they were dealing with right then. They had wanted God to give them a ruler for their nation and instead, God gave them a ruler for their hearts. They were thinking about the moment, and God was thinking about forever.

Bible Verse:

The Bible verse today comes from **Mark 11:8**. You say after me: **"Many in the crowd passed out their coats before Jesus, while others threw down palm branches."**

Those people wanted to crucify Jesus by the end of the week because Jesus wasn't what they had asked for. They couldn't see that God had sent them a king who was so much more, so much greater than any king they could ever have wished for. They were too small-minded to see the big picture.

Sometimes our greatest gifts from God are when he says No. God sees the big picture. He's got the whole world in his hands.

Sermon Ending:

I brought each of you a little chocolate world today. I hope it will help you remember that God has the whole world in his hands.

Devotional Ending:

Keep your eyes, your ears, and your heart open to God. Remember that he sees the big picture and has your "forever" in the palm of his hand.

Prayer:

Now, bow you head, close your eyes, and let's talk to God. You say after me: **"Dear God, Thank you for saying yes to my prayers and for when you say no. Amen."**

(I was able to find chocolate balls wrapped in foil with a world map printed on them at World Market. If you cannot find those, the Oriental Trading Catalog has 2" earth squeeze balls, sold by the dozen. As a last resort, use small blue balls or large marbles.)

#92
A Kiss For Silver
Based on Luke 22
(Easter Sunday)

THEME: No amount of money is worth more than love.

I want to talk to you about a kiss today. A kiss is meant to be something sweet. A kiss is meant to show someone you care about them and love them. A kiss is a very special thing. But the kiss I want to tell you about today was one that was terrible and sad, and it changed the world. One kiss changed the world!

You have heard that Jesus had twelve disciples. They were the twelve who followed him, believed in him, and loved him. One of those disciples was named Judas, and Judas loved money. He loved money more than he loved Jesus. Perhaps because of that, he was an easy target for the devil. The devil crept right into the heart of Judas and convinced him to sell Jesus to the men who hated him and wanted him dead.

Judas went to those men and said he would turn Jesus over to them for thirty silver coins. They agreed and followed Judas to the place where Jesus and the other disciples were. Judas had told those men that the person he walked up to and kissed on the cheek would be Jesus. And so Judas did walk up to Jesus, and he did kiss him on the cheek, and those men arrested Jesus.

Thirty silver coins for the life of God's son. . . *(presenter should slowly pour 30 silver coins — silver dollars, Susan B. Anthony dollars, half dollars, or quarters — out of a pouch and into an attractive coffee can so it will make a lot of noise.)* Oh, how sad when we love money more than we love Jesus.

Bible Verse:

The Bible verse today comes from Luke **22:48**. You say after me: **"Jesus said, 'Judas, how can you do this — betray me with a kiss?'"**

As God often does, he used something bad and turned it into something good. Even though the kiss from Judas got Jesus captured and crucified, Jesus suffered on that cross and died so that you and I could reach God. Miraculously, Jesus rose from the dead and lives in heaven with God, but more importantly, he lives here on earth in our hearts.

If you could walk up to Jesus, what kind of kiss would you give him — a kiss for love or a kiss for silver?

Sermon Ending:

I have a chocolate kiss for you this Easter morning to go along with one of these silver coins. When you eat your kiss, I hope it will remind you of the Judas kiss and how he sold out Jesus for money. I want you to always keep your coin to help you remember that no amount of money in the world is worth more than love.

Devotional Ending:

Make all your kisses special, and give them with love. Never use one to hurt somebody the way Judas hurt Jesus.

Prayer:

Now, bow your head, close your eyes, and let's talk to God. You say after me: **"Dear God, Give Jesus a kiss of love for me.**

Amen."

(Use Hershey's chocolate kisses. The children are familiar with them and recognize them as "kisses.")

#93
The Lamb Of God
Based on I Peter 1:13
(Easter Sunday)

THEME: Easter is about new life from death.

It looks like to me some of you are wearing new Easter clothes. There is a reason why people wear new clothes on Easter Sunday. *New clothes are a symbol of new life,* and the custom comes from the Easter Sunday baptism of Christians a long, long time ago who were let into church wearing new robes.

I am sure some of you have heard of the Easter Bunny. Well, bunny rabbits have lots of babies, *so the rabbit became an Easter symbol of new life. Eggs also represent new life,* and Christians adopted the egg as an Easter symbol because of the relationship between Easter and the renewal of life. They were painted with colors to represent the sunlight of spring.

Easter lilies are used to decorate at Easter time because of their pure white blossoms that *remind Christians of the pure new life* that comes to us through the resurrection of Jesus. The resurrection of Jesus means that after he died on the cross, he did not stay dead. He rose up and came back to life.

There is one more Easter symbol I want to tell you about, and that is the lamb. All the other things I have told you about symbolize new life, but the lamb is different. *The lamb represents death.* You see, a lamb was sacrificed, killed, the night that the Angel of Death took the lives of Egypt's first born sons. But anyone who had lamb's blood smeared across their door, was passed over by the death angel. From that event came the word **Passover**. The Passover lamb's blood saved lives. When Jesus died on the cross, his blood saved our lives, and that is why Christians call Jesus the Lamb of God.

Bible Verse:

Our Bible verse today comes from **I Peter 1:13**. You say after me: **"He paid for you with the precious lifeblood of Christ, the sinless and spotless Lamb of God."**

As I was studying for the lesson this week, I was thinking how wonderful it would be if I could have arranged for Jesus to walk through that front/back door so that you could see him, touch him, smell him, and hear him, and then I realized that Jesus would already be here. He would be in your eyes, your smile, your touch, your voice, your breath, and your heart. *(If there is more than one child, point to or touch different children as you say the preceding part.)* You see, Jesus lives in every Christian. He lives! That is what Easter is all about: *new life from death.*

I want you to remember the lamb and this Easter Sunday when you learned that Easter isn't just about Easter egg hunts, lilies, new clothes, and a bunny. It is about the Lamb of God, Jesus, who died and rose from the dead so that we could be children of God forever.

Sermon Ending:

I have a lamb for each of you to remind you of Jesus' death, and I have an egg to symbolize new life that we received when he rose from the dead.

Devotional Ending:
Share Jesus with others who don't know him so that they can receive new life from his death and resurrection. Jesus is the most precious gift you can give.

Prayer:
Now, bow your head, close your eyes, and let's pray. You say after me: **"Dear Jesus, Thank you for being our sacrificial lamb and for giving us eternal life. Amen."**

(I made the lambs using a pattern out of the book "Bible Fun For Everyone." This book has several patterns and ideas in it that I used for different sermons/lessons. See my introductions on where to find this book.)

(I used colored plastic eggs and put a piece of Easter candy inside each one. I put an Easter sticker on the outside of each egg.)

#94

Pentecost
Based on Acts 2:1-6, 25
(Pentecost Sunday)

THEME: Allow the Holy Spirit to keep you fired up in faith.

This is Pentecost Sunday. Back in the Bible days when Moses was alive, God told Moses to announce to the people of Israel that they were to celebrate several yearly festivals of the Lord, special times when they were to meet together and worship God, and there were certain rules to these celebrations they were to follow. One of those celebrations or festivals was called Pentecost, and it was to be held fifty days after the Passover celebration.

Year after year the people celebrated Pentecost, but the year that Jesus was crucified and then rose from the dead, something spectacular happened. It's a story from the Bible I want you to hear. It's an incredible story, but it really happened. It is from the Book of Acts, chapter 2.

It was the day of Pentecost, and people who believed in Jesus, the Christians, were meeting together. Suddenly there was a sound like the roaring of a mighty windstorm in the skies above them, and it filled the house where they were meeting. Then what looked like flames or tongues of fire appeared and settled on top of their heads! Everyone there became filled with the Holy Spirit and began speaking in languages they didn't even know.

Since it was Pentecost, there were lots of people in Jerusalem that day from many different countries for the festival, and when they heard the roaring in the sky above the house where the Christians were meeting, they rushed over. To there amazement, they heard the Christians speaking in all of their different native languages, telling about the miracles of God.

They saw the tongues of fire dancing on top of their heads and all around them, and they witnessed first-hand the Holy Spirit of God. Many of those people who had not believed in Jesus before became Christians that day. Different kinds of people who spoke all different kinds of languages became the first converts to Christianity.

Bible Verse:

The Bible verse today comes from **Acts 2:25**. You say after me: **"I know the Lord is always with me. He is helping me. God's mighty power supports me."**

The same Holy Spirit that changed the hearts of those people on that day of Pentecost is the very same Holy Spirit that is with us on this day of Pentecost. God and Jesus are with us now and forever.

Sermon Ending:

I brought each of you a boomerang today. It is a toy that you throw, and it comes back to you. It is to remind you that even if you run away from God, he is always there for you to come back to.

Devotional Ending:

Allow the Holy Spirit to keep you fired up in your faith. Ask Jesus to keep your heart pure, and be forever mindful of God's power. God's love is like a boomerang. Even if you run away from God, he is always there for you to come back to.

Prayer:

Now, bow your head, close your eyes, and let's talk to God. You say after me: **"Dear God, I pray that others will be able to see your Holy Spirit working in me. Amen."**

(I found small plastic boomerangs in the party favors section of Dollar Tree. Many toy stores have them. The Oriental Trading Catalog *has several different varieties.)*

#95
Soul Custody
Based on Matthew 3:13-17
(on the meaning of baptism and The Trinity)

THEME: The Trinity — the team that adopts your soul.

I want to talk to you about baptism today. Baptism is an agreement between God and us where we promise to give God our soul, and God promises to keep our soul clean. The water for baptism is the visible thing we use to seal that agreement with God. The water represents the blood of Jesus, and it symbolizes a way to clean us up from our sins — the things we do wrong. The water all by itself doesn't actually clean up our souls. It is our promise to let Jesus lead our lives that does that.

God has three different ways to take care of our soul when we become Christians. He has himself, the Father we pray to and worship. He has his son, Jesus, the Light of the World, and the third way is through the Holy Spirit. It is through the Holy Spirit that we can feel God here on earth. It is that spirit that seeps into our soul and connects us with God and Jesus.

When a person is baptized, God gives them his Holy Spirit,

he gives them Jesus, and he gives them himself — all three in one. That is quite a team! It is that team that adopts your soul.

When Jesus lived on earth, he didn't need to be baptized, but he did it anyway to show people that the act of baptism is important, because it shows a person's desire to become one of God's children. After Jesus was baptized, the Bible says that God opened up heaven and sent down his Holy Spirit to Jesus in the form of a dove to show how pleased he was, and that is what our Bible verse is about today.

Bible Verse:

The Bible verse comes from **Matthew 3:16**. You say after me: **"After Jesus' baptism, . . . the heavens were opened to him, and he saw the spirit of God coming down in the form of a dove."**

Baptism is not a requirement for God's promise. It is a gift of God's promise. In other words — God doesn't say we have to be baptized, he lets us be baptized as a way to physically reach out and adopt us into his kingdom. His promise meant so much to him, that he sealed it, not with water, but with the blood of his own son.

Sermon Ending:

I brought each of you a white candle in the form of a dove. The candle is for Jesus, who saved your soul from darkness. The dove represents the Holy Spirit who nourishes your soul, and the white stands for God's pure and cleansing love for your soul.

Devotional Ending:

Jesus saves your soul, the Holy Spirit nourishes your soul, and God adopts your soul. You just can't lose with a team like that!

Prayer:

Now, bow your head, close your eyes, and let's talk to God. You say after me: **"Dear God, my heavenly Father, Thank you for the team that will adopt my soul. Amen."**

(I went to town to find either birthday candles for the rebirth of

baptism, or little white doves to represent the Holy Spirit coming down to Jesus in the form of a dove. I went to the Card and Party Factory, a store in our small town, and looked in the wedding section. To my astonishment, I found small white candles in the form of a dove, and they came five to a package. I do not know why I still get so surprised when God leads me to the perfect token/gift/treat for my church children. What a blessing! What a God!)

#96
Thanksgiving, What's That About?
Based on I Chronicles 16:8
(Thanksgiving season)

THEME: Be aware of your blessings, and then be thankful.

A long time ago, almost 400 years ago, some people in England got tired of being told how to worship God. So, they got on a ship called The Mayflower, and sailed to America. They ended up at a place they called Plymouth. England was very far away from America — all the way across the ocean. Since they made this pilgrimage — a pilgrimage is a long trip to a new place — they called themselves Pilgrims.

The weather in Plymouth was very cold, and about half of them died. If it hadn't been for the Indians who helped them, they would probably all have died.

There is an old legend about five kernels of corn that says some days the Pilgrims had only enough food for each person to have five kernels of corn to eat for the whole day. *(Presenter needs to show children some dry kernels of corn.)* However, the Indians taught them how to hunt and fish and grow corn and other vegetables, and by the next autumn, the Pilgrims had enough food for everyone. They invited their Indian friends over for their feast of thanksgiving.

The legend has it that when Thanksgiving time came around again, the Pilgrims put five kernels of corn on each plate to remind themselves of their blessings:

1. One kernel was to remind them of the autumn beauty all around them.
2. Another kernel represented their love for one another.
3. A third kernel symbolized God's love and care for them.
4. The fourth kernel stood for their Indian friends.
5. And the last kernel reminded them of their freedom to worship God as they chose.

Bible Verse:

Our Bible verse today comes from **I Chronicles 16:8**. You say after me: **"Oh, give thanks to the Lord and pray to him."**

Sermon Ending:

Many of the traditional things we eat on Thanksgiving Day are the same foods the Pilgrims and Indians ate on that first Thanksgiving, like turkey and corn for example. I couldn't bring each of you a turkey, but I did bring you some candy corn in a Thanksgiving jar. Every time you eat a kernel of it, I want you to thank God for one of your blessings, like your mom or dad, or your house, or your pet, or even for your bed. You have so many things to be thankful for.

Devotional Ending:

Perhaps this Thanksgiving you could ask your mom or dad to get some dried corn from a feed store, or even some candy corn, and put five kernels of it on everyone's plate. Ask each one at the table to name five of their blessings before you begin eating your Thanksgiving dinner, and then thank God for them all.

Prayer:

Now, bow your head, close your eyes, and let's talk to God.

You say after me: "**Dear God, We are thankful for our many blessings. Keep us aware of them. Amen.**"

(You may put the candy corn in any container, however, I bought some little plastic containers and glued stringed sequins around the top to make them sparkle. Children love sparkle, and presentation makes the difference between a good lesson and a GREAT lesson.)

#97
Giving God Some Thanks
Based on Luke 17:11-19 and Psalms 92:1
(Thanksgiving season)

THEME: Do you remember to say, "Thank you, God?"

I want you to think about the word **Thanksgiving** for a minute. If you turn it around it would be giving thanks. Giving thanks. Out of all the things people give to each other and to God, the easiest and least expensive is thanks. Sadly, thanks is not something we frequently give to God.

(Presenter may want to substitute something more appropriate to them for this paragraph.) Just this morning someone said, "My, that is a pretty hat." I said, "Thank you." When I go to the grocery store and the grocery checker gives me the receipt for my groceries, I say, "Thank you." When I come home from work and it's my husband's day off, and he has cleaned the house, I say, "Thank you, Sweetheart." If someone holds a door open for me, I say, "Thank you," and I truly mean it when I say those two very important words. There are days that I probably say thank you dozens of times, but while working on this lesson, I realized that

Goldfish and Silver Kisses

I don't say thank you to God nearly as often as I do to people I don't even know, and God gave me the air that I breathe, the earth that I live on, the love in my heart. God gave me Jesus. God gave me life, and there have been days that I didn't take the time to just say, "Thank you, God."

I go to God to pray and to ask for his blessings and his protection and his help. He wants us to come to him with our problems — with everything. God is always there for us, but we need to remember to thank God every single day. It doesn't cost anything. It is not hard to do. It is a simple thing, but oh, how it pleases God when we take the time to give him some thanks.

Bible Verse:

The Bible verse today comes from **Psalms 92:1**. You say after me: "**It is good to say, 'Thank you' to the Lord.**"

Thanksgiving Day is coming Thursday. It is a holiday where we will celebrate with family and friends. On a lot of tables there will be turkey and dressing, all kinds of vegetables and breads, and maybe even pumpkin or pecan pie. We will visit and **eat**, play and **eat**, watch football and parades and **eat**, but let's remember to do one more thing. Let's remember to give thanks to God. That is what Thanksgiving is about.

We need to remember to thank whoever provided the wonderful meal, thank people for coming over, thank each other for hugs they give us. That is all important, but the most important thing to do is to give thanks to God for all our many blessings.

Sermon Ending:

I brought each of you a Thanksgiving card and a marker. Between now and Thursday, write down or draw things that you need to thank God for. On Thanksgiving Day, right before it is time to eat, share your list with God, and give him your thanks. Try to remember to thank God everyday.

Devotional Ending:

Between now and Thursday, write down or draw things that

you need to thank God for. On Thanksgiving Day, right before it is time to eat, share your list with God, and give him your thanks. Try to remember to thank God everyday.

Prayer:

Now, bow your head, close your eyes, and let's talk to God. You say after me: **"Dear God, Thank you for all you do for me. I love you. Amen."**

(You can buy Thanksgiving cards, but I took stiff orange paper and put a Thanksgiving sticker on each sheet. Holiday stickers can even be bought at grocery stores.)

#98

In The Names Of Jesus
Based on John 18:33-37 and Daniel 7:14
(Christ the King Sunday or anytime)

THEME: Let Jesus be your "life-saver."

I want to talk to you about something that everyone has. It is something important to you. It is something that defines you and tells people who you are. It is your name, and it was given to you when you were born.

A very special baby was born over 2000 years ago, and he was given a name. He was given the name Jesus, but as he grew up, he was given many more names, names that describe who he was and who he is. One of those names is Counselor because he gives the right advice. He has been called The Son of Man because of his humanity. He's also known as the Light of the World because light is a symbol for truth. He is called The Good Shepherd because of his love and guidance. Jesus has been referred to as The Way, The Truth, and The Life because he is the method and message and the meaning for all people.

We can call Jesus Lord, The All Powerful One, the Son of

God, and the Lamb of God. We call Jesus: Christ, Redeemer, King of Kings, and Lord of Lords. We can call him the Morning Star, but for Jesus to make a difference in your life, you have to know him by the name of Savior. It means that you believe that he died on a rugged cross to save you from the mistakes and the things you do wrong in this life. Jesus, the Savior, paid for your ticket into heaven. He is your "life-saver."

Bible Verse:

The Bible verse today comes from **Daniel 7:14**. You say after me: **"His power is eternal, it will never end, his government shall never fall."**

Jesus is real; he will never go away. So, no matter what you call him whether it is Teacher, Messiah, or Prince of Peace, make sure that you know him as Savior. Make Jesus the King of your heart and your life. Make him your life-saver.

Sermon Ending:

Have you ever noticed that a Life-Saver candy is in the shape of a life-saver like those that are thrown into the water to save someone from drowning? Well, I brought each of you a roll of Life-Savers today to help you remember that Jesus is a "life-saver," and he can save you from drowning in a life of sin and wrong-doing. He has paved your way into heaven.

Devotional Ending:

(Presenter should hold up a roll of original flavored Life-Savers.) Have you ever noticed that a Life-Saver candy is in the shape of a life-saver like those that are thrown into the water to save someone from drowning? The next time you get a roll of Life-Savers, I hope you will remember that Jesus is a "life-saver," and he can save you from drowning in a life of sin and wrong doing. He has paved your way into heaven.

Prayer:

Now, bow your head, close your eyes, and let's talk to Jesus. You say after me: **"Dear Jesus, Be my teacher, be my king, be**

my savior. Amen."

(I suggest getting the original flavored rolls of Life-Savers. Children like them better than the wintergreen or peppermint flavors, and the package is more colorful and recognizable.)

#99

Bittersweet
Based on Hebrews 5:4
(for when a pastor is leaving/retiring)

THEME: Saying good-by.
    I want to teach you an odd sort of word today. That word is BITTERSWEET. It is made up of two separate words — bitter and sweet — and they mean the exact opposite of each other. Something bitter is tart tasting, or it can mean sad or unpleasant; something sweet is good and pleasing. So when we say BITTERSWEET, we are expressing the idea that something is sad — or bad — and good at the same time or tart tasting and sweet tasting at the same time.
    How many of you like chocolate chip cookies? Well, the chocolate chips in a chocolate chip cookie are bittersweet. They are tart and sweet all at the same time to make them taste just the way they should.
    I wanted to talk about the word bittersweet today because this is a bittersweet day in our church. It is a sad, bitter day, because it is Pastor (Boyd's) last Sunday to be our pastor.

Goldfish and Silver Kisses

However, it is a good day, a sweet day, because we know that Pastor (Boyd) is retiring after many years of hard work, and he deserves a rest form his labor. [**Optional:** . . . is moving to a new church where he is needed and can serve God there like he has served God here.]

As Christians, we must learn to put aside our feelings of sadness and replace them with feelings of joy when a person we love makes changes that are good for them. When we do that, it pleases God.

Bible Verse:

The Bible verse today comes from **Hebrews 5:4**. You say after me. "**There is a full complete rest waiting for the people of God.**"

Pastor (Boyd) has spent/spends his life serving God and serving God's people. He has spent/spends his life teaching people how to become and live as Christians. He has encouraged us to **see the good** in others, to **speak nicely** about others, and to choose to **hear what is good** about others, rather than listening for the bad. Because of Pastor (Boyd's) desire and commitment to let God work through him, the world we live in is a better place. So, even though we are sad that he will no longer be our pastor, we are happy and grateful for the time he spent here with us.

Prayer:

Bow your head, close your eyes, and let's talk to God. You say after me: "**Dear God, Please bless Pastor (Boyd.) Thank you for sharing him with us. Amen.**"

I want to give each of you the opportunity to say a special "good-by" to Pastor (Boyd) and give him one last treat as a bittersweet reminder of us. *(I always give the pastor whatever I give the children.)* Each of you take two chocolate chip cookies. Give one to Pastor (Boyd) and the other one is for you to keep as a reminder of this bittersweet day in our church. If you like, you may also give Pastor (Boyd) a hug with his cookie. I think he would like that.

Devotional Ending:

Be sure to say a special "good-by" to Pastor (Boyd,) and give him a hug to help him remember this bittersweet day in our church. I think he would like that.

(God always helps me find the perfect treat for my church children, so I was not surprised when I found the perfect cookie jar for our pastor. It was blue with a coconut tree on it. Coconuts were on the top of the lid. The perfect thing about it was the three monkeys across the front. They were the "see no evil, speak no evil, and hear no evil" monkeys, and it went right along with the message in the sermon. Thanks God!)

#100
Gone Fishing
Based on Matthew 4:18-22
(can be used for a pastor's first Sunday in your church)

THEME: Jesus has a fishing job for you.

Our scriptures today come from the book of Matthew where he tells us the story about where Jesus found his first four disciples. There names were Peter, Andrew, James and John. Those guys were at work when Jesus came along to recruit them. They didn't have high paying or real important jobs, and they weren't extra special or famous people that everybody looked up to. They were just plain ordinary men, with plain ordinary jobs. In fact, they all had the same kind of job. Do you know what their jobs were? They were fishermen.

Have any of you ever been fishing? If you have, you probably found out that if you spend all day at it, you get dirty and smelly. That was the shape those four guys were in when Jesus found them. They were dirty and smelled like fish, but Jesus looked beyond all that and saw what kind of men they were on the inside. You see, Jesus was looking for men who had a clean heart, men that would help others no matter what the cost — men who loved God.

Jesus called for Peter and Andrew, James and John to quit their jobs right then and there and follow him. Jesus told them that he had a new job for them. They would still be fishermen, but instead of fishing for fish, they would fish for men's souls.

A person's soul is their spirit, their love, and their thoughts. Your soul is the part of you that lives on after your body dies. It is the part of you that God has invited to heaven if you let Jesus be your guide.

Did you know that Jesus wants all of us to be fishermen like Peter, Andrew, James, and John. Not the kind that fishes for fish, but the kind that fishes or looks for people who need help finding God.

Bible Verse:

The Bible verse today comes from **Matthew 4:19**. You say after me: **"Jesus called out, 'Come along with me, and I will show you how to fish for the souls of men.'"**

There is someone new to our church today who obeyed Jesus like those first four disciples did. He had a job in another place preaching, but our church needed a new preacher, so he obeyed the call to come here and fish for souls. He is our new pastor, and his name is Pastor (Bruce.) In a minute I want you to meet him and for him to meet you, but first let's talk to God.

Prayer:

Bow your heads and close your eyes. You say after me: **"Dear God, Help me to fish for souls and place them in your care. Amen."**

Sermon Ending:

I brought each of you two bags of Gold Fish crackers today. Give one to Pastor (Bruce) as a thank you for coming here. Keep the other one as a reminder that Jesus has a fishing job for you.

Devotional Ending:

Give Pastor (Bruce) a hug and thank him for coming here. And don't forget, God has a fishing job for you.

(Give the pastor an old-fashioned fish bowl so he will have something to put his bags of fish in. I used the giant-sized pizza flavored and cheddar flavored Gold Fish crackers. The two flavors are slightly different in color, making it more attractive. You will probably want to put around ten 10-14 crackers in each bag.)

#101
9 - 1 - 1
*Based on Romans 5:1-11
(terrorist attack on America)*

(This lesson is in memory and in honor of those who lost their lives or their loved ones during the Attack on America, September 11, 2001.)

THEME: God's power is behind America because his son lives in the hearts of America.

This has been a very sad week for our country, the United States of America. Some evil men flew jet airplanes into some very important buildings killing thousands of innocent people. You may wonder why God would let that happen. The truth is, God gave us something very special when he made man-kind. He gave us a human nature — free will to think what we want to and the right to choose whether or not we love people or God. And with those freedoms come differences. You see, different kinds of people have different opinions about life, love, what's good or evil, and even God.

Since the very first people on earth, God watched as some

human nature turned evil, but instead of giving up on man-kind, he gave us another gift, and his name is Jesus.

The evil men who attacked our country didn't and don't believe in Jesus. They don't understand his power, his love, or his purpose. But we do, and that is what will help us overcome the horrors of this past week. You see, God, along with the love and inspiration of Jesus within us, often does his greatest work in the worst of times. Like last Friday people all over America stopped what they were doing and prayed to God, and then I saw on the news that it wasn't just Americans praying, it was people all over the world, thousands upon thousands, praying *for* America. And you know what? God was listening.

Bible Verse:

The Bible verse today comes from **Romans 5:4**. You say after me: "**Endurance develops strength of character in us.**"

That means that life's tough situations bring out the best in people, and the best in people is where Jesus lives.

Our nation, our world turned to God this past week, and he has heard us. Those prayers have brought people of all races and religions to a place where our differences just don't seem to matter that much, and we are seeing what is really important; that is the precious gift God gave us of freedom — our human nature.

Sermon Ending:

I brought each of you an American flag clip to wear because this week our flag has come to mean more than just a symbol for America, it has become a banner for the world as a symbol of unity, freedom, and faith in God. Believe that God's power is behind America because his son, Jesus, lives in the hearts of America.

Devotional Ending:

This week our flag has come to mean more than just a symbol for America, it has become a banner for the world as a symbol of unity, freedom, and faith in God. Believe that God's power is behind America because his son, Jesus, lives in the hearts of America.

Prayer:

Now, bow your head, close your eyes, and let's talk to God. You say after me: "**Dear God, Comfort our sadness, strengthen our spirits, and God, bless America. Amen.**"

(The American Flag clips came from the Oriental Trading Catalog.*)*

About The Author . . .

Linda Carol Masters grew up in the small East Texas town of Corrigan. She attended Baylor, Stephen F. Austin, and Sam Houston State Universities, graduating in 1978. Linda, a wife and mother, taught second grade for eight years before teaching inmates in a maximum security state penitentiary for the Windham School District where she is currently employed. Her life-long dream and passion has been to write. This is her first book.

www.ingramcontent.com/pod-product-compliance
Lightning Source LLC
Chambersburg PA
CBHW032036150426
43194CB00006B/299